Wordpress In A Week ...Or Less

Zak Cagaros

CONTENTS

INTRODUCTION	2
HOW YOU SHOULD USE THIS BOOK	2
MONDAY	3
Chapter 1: The Easy Way To Build Websites	3
What is WordPress?	3
Features of Word press	4
WordPress.org vs. WordPress.com	5
Why choose WordPress?	6
Coca Cola France	8
Sony Music	8
The New York Times	10
How to find out if a website is using WordPress	10
What you will need	11
A domain name	11
Your domain name should be your website name	11
Your domain name should match your brand name	11
Get a short meaningful domain name	11
Including "the", and "my" in your domain name	12
A web host	12
Reliability and speed of access	12
Data transfer	12
Disk space	13
Technical support	13
Make sure to avoid resellers	13
Chapter 2: Getting Wordpress Up and Running	14
The Famous 5 Minute Installation	14
QuickInstall	14
Fantastico	16
Chapter 3: Getting To Know Wordpress	19

The frontend as the user sees it — 19

How to log into WordPress backend — 20

How to change your password — 20

Your workspace: The Dashboard — 21

The Side Bar — 23
- 1. Posts — 23
- How to publish a new Post — 23
- 2. Media — 24
- 3. Pages — 24
- How to publish a page — 24
- 4. Comments — 25
- 5. Appearance — 25
- 6. Plug-ins — 26
- 7. Users — 27
- 8. Tools — 27
- 9. Settings — 27
- Update notifications — 27
- Screen options — 28

Change basic settings — 29

Writing Settings — 31

Reading Settings — 32

Discussion settings — 33
- Default article settings — 33
- Comment settings — 34
- Avatars — 35

Media settings — 36

Permalinks — 36

Remove sample content — 37
- Delete the "Hello World" Post — 37
- Delete sample page — 38
- Remove Widgets — 39

Plan your site — 41

TUESDAY — 43

Chapter 4: Creating Killer Content — 43

How to Create Posts — 43

How to show part of a post as a preview	45
How to Create a Sticky Post	46
Updating a post	47
Post publishing options: Delayed publishing	47
Categories: Organizing Your Content	**48**
How to create a category	48
How to assign a post to a category	50
Tags	50
How to add Tags to your posts	51
Using Clean URLs	**52**
Long post titles	54
Pages	**54**
Pages v Posts	55
How to create pages	56
Comments	**59**
Moderating comments	59
How to leave a comment	60
Preventing comment spam	63
Avatar	64
Chapter 5: Creating an Attractive Website With Themes	**66**
Install custom header for your theme	67
Customize theme background	69
Customization menu	70
The theme editor	71
How to download and install a new theme	71
Free themes v Premium themes	76
Widgets	**77**
Widget settings	77
Core widgets	**79**
Categories	79
Custom Menu	80
Links	80
Pages	80
Recent Comments & Recent Posts	80
Search	80
Text	80

Help your visitors find what they want: Creating Menus	80
Add Links and Categories to Menu	83

WEDNESDAY 85

Chapter 6: Getting More Out of Your Site With Wordpress Plugins — 85

How to install and manage plug-ins — 85

How to find good plug-ins — 88

Enhancing your website using core plug-ins — 90
- SEO Plug-in — 90
- Anti-Spam Plug-in — 90
- Backup Plug-in — 90
- Contact Plug-in — 90
- Captcha Plug-in — 90
- Sharebar Plug-in — 90
- Group related posts Plug-in — 91
- Speed up the load process Plug-in — 91
- Re-use old content Plug-in — 91

Premium plug-ins — 91

Chapter 7: Bring Your Content to Life — 92

The Media Library — 92

How to upload media — 93

How to create great looking posts — 96
- The formatting toolbar — 96
- Add media — 96
- Bold, italic, strikethrough and lists — 97
- Block quote, horizontal line and alignment — 97
- Insert links, create snippets and writing mode — 97
- Paragraph — 98
- Text color, justify, paste, and clear formatting — 98
- Special characters — 99
- Indent, undo/redo, and help — 99
- HTML and Visual view — 100

Post format — 100
- Standard — 100
- Aside — 101
- Image — 101
- Link — 101
- Quote — 101
- Status — 101

How to add pictures to posts — 101

Featured image	104
How to divide a post into multiple pages	105
Static v Dynamic sites	106
Home page: static or blog?	107
What are Embeds and Shortcodes?	107
How to embed video into a post	107
Shortcodes	109
How to create a gallery	109
Chapter 8: Open Up Your Site & Enable Users to Log In & Contribute	112
How to add users to your site	113
Collaborate with authors	115
Get readers to share your content	117
How to add Share buttons to your content	118
Chapter 9: Keep Things Running By Securing Your Site	123
Back up WordPress	123
Use strong passwords	124
Keep WordPress up to date	124
Keep plug-ins up to date	124
Password protect your WP-admin folder	124
Hide your plug-ins	124
Install limit login attempts	124

FRIDAY 125

Chapter 10: Attracting Search Engine Traffic	125
The importance of accommodating for search engines	125
Optimize your articles	125
Use clear formatting	126
Write Pillar content	126

Ask your readers — 126

Be unique and controversial — 127

Images — 127

Body content — 127

Guest posting — 127

Comment on other sites — 128
- Comment on related sites — 128
- Comment early — 128
- Use a good opening sentence — 128
- Disagree — 128
- Good spelling, grammar and format — 128
- Comment regularly — 128

Use social media — 129
- Facebook — 129
- Twitter — 129
- Google plus — 130
- YouTube — 130

Link your posts internally — 131

Monitoring Site visitors — 133

Chapter 11: Practical Tips To Create A Successful Blog — 137

Find your passion — 137

Do your homework: keyword Research — 138
- Supply — 139
- Demand — 140

Long Tail Keywords — 141

Come up with solutions and you will be successful — 142
- How to identify problems to solve — 142

Write a list post — 142

Write eye catching headlines — 142

Use benefit rich statements — 142

Ask a question — 143

Add humor — 143

Incorporate the word 'you' into your content — 143

Add real life and personal events	143
Hold contests	143
Learn from the pros	143

CONCLUSION — 144

MORE WORDPRESS RESOURCES — 145

Introduction

The method of Do-It-Yourself (DIY) has been around for a long time, and in majority of the cases this has been associated with home renovation and make overs. But, in the past decade this mindset of DIY has shifted to the online world. It has now become the norm for anyone to create their own website without seeking the help of a website professional, this has been made possible with platforms like Wordpress. Since this is a relatively new phenomenon, beginners need someone to guide them through the many different and confusing paths they need to traverse to create the website that they want. My name is Zak Cagaros and I have been creating websites since 2003, and I would like to help you in your quest to create your own website without breaking the bank! In this book you will learn in the most clearest of terms, how to create a fully functional website in the space of several hours – without compromising on quality. One of the main reasons I wrote this book was because I was frustrated at seeing hundreds of books that promised beginners to Wordpress that they would learn everything they needed to build a website, only to find that the content of the book does not deliver on this promise. I believe that basic education on how to create a website using this great platform should be extremely affordable if not free, because we are now in the 21st century, also called the information age, and you need to learn new skills and make sure that you keep updating your skills to stay abreast.

How you should use this book

There are 11 chapters in this book that go into detail about all aspects of Wordpress that beginners need to know. This book is best utilized by reading all the chapters first, the approximate word count is 38,000, and so it shouldn't take you too long to read. Then, you can come back to specific chapters that you want to focus on, but I am confident that by the time you are through with this book you will have a fully functional website, and you will be confident enough to progress onto more advanced topics in Wordpress, which will help you to take your website to the next level. I know you are excited at the prospect of creating your own website, so, without further ado onto chapter one!

Monday

Chapter 1: The Easy Way To Build Websites

No more webpages! Embrace the online revolution. Building a website the traditional way involves creating HTML documents – webpages one by one. As the site grows, you'd end up with several HTML documents and you'd have to keep all of them organized and make sure all menu links stay up-to-date. You would maintain the website by yourself, because it is hard for other people to learn their way around the structure of your particular site, or to become proficient in the web editing software you used. This is where a Content Management System (CMS) really becomes the tool to use for creating a website. A CMS is an application that runs on a web server. It allows you to develop and maintain a website online, and it comes packed with features, ranging from basic features to modify content to advanced functionality such as user registration and site search capability. In other words, a CMS makes it possible to build sites that would normally be created by a full team of web professionals such as programmers and front end Web developers. Also, creating websites without a CMS would involve spending large amounts of money, time and resources. A CMS employs advanced scripts that use a database to store the content of your website. The CMS would retrieve information from the database and present it in the form of webpages.

The dynamic nature of storing and presenting content makes a CMS extremely flexible - you can show only a selection of articles from a specific category; you can display only the intro texts of the most recent posts on the homepage; you can have a list of links to the most popular content; you can limit access to registered users only; and you can do all of these things just by using a CMS, without writing a single line of code. Furthermore, the CMS allows you to integrate all sorts of extra features, including contact forms, picture galleries, and much more. The best part of a content management system is that it is open source software. This means that it is distributed free of charge and more importantly unlocked, unlike commercial software. Because it is open source and freely available, other software developers are encouraged to modify and to help improve the CMS. This means that the CMS is constantly being improved and supported by a global community of developers.

What is WordPress?

WordPress is a Content Management System that you can download free and use to create a full-blown website. WordPress was first released on May 27 2003, by Matt Mullenweg and Mike Little. WordPress was originally created for blogging but as with the advent of plug-ins (software scripts to extend WordPress), you can use WordPress to create almost any kind of website. Like most CMS's, WordPress is open source which means that you can download and even modify the code under the hood for your own use without having to pay for it like traditional software.

One of the main features that make WordPress such a popular CMS is the wide array of available plug-ins that you can add to your WordPress website that will dramatically enhance its functionality. So if you decide to sell on your website, then you can get a plug-in that will do just that for you and you can be selling from your website in minutes!

Features of Word press

As of the time of this writing WordPress is used as the platform to power 20% of all websites on the Internet; these include simple websites, blogs, portals, and large corporation websites. Because WordPress is simple for users and publishers, it is increasing in popularity every day and will only get better. Some of the features of WordPress include:

- Simplicity - this is the main reason why WordPress is such a popular content management system, because it makes it possible for you to get online and get publishing quickly. You can have a website up and running with WordPress in 60 minutes or less.
- Theme system - WordPress has changed the way websites are created forever. You can create a totally new look and feel to your website by simply installing a new theme with a click of a button. In addition, you have a selection of free and quality WordPress themes to choose from.
- Extend the functionality of your website - the beautiful thing with WordPress is that you are not limited to the default installation of WordPress. For almost every feature that you can think of is a plug-in that you can add to your website to extend its functionality. For example, to sell products on your website all you have to do is add a plug-in that will enable your website to list products, add images and check out functionality to your website. Plug-ins are pieces of code that have been specially written for a specific purpose and they will easily add extended functionality to your website. But, best of all is that most of the plug-ins are absolutely free!
- Limitless Functionality – with the ability to extend the functionality of your website, you can create practically any type of website that you want: personal blog or website, photo blog, business website, professional portfolio, news website, and many other types of websites.
- Priceless Value! Now, one might think that it would cost you an arm and a leg to use WordPress, but because WordPress is licensed under the GPL license scheme, it means that you are free to use WordPress in any way you choose. This means that you can install it, use it for any purpose you want, add to it, modify it and even distribute it.

WordPress.org vs. WordPress.com

You might have heard of WordPress.com as well as WordPress.org, and you're wondering: what is the difference between them? Briefly, WordPress.org is where the software is freely available to download along with thousands of free plug-ins. This is the place where you would download the Wordpress software and you would install it yourself. WordPress.com on the other hand uses the same software, but it focuses on the provision of hosting services. This means that if you choose to have a website on WordPress.com it will be hosted for you but you do not exclusively own all of your content! So if you sign up with WordPress.com you will have a website like: yourwebistename.WordPress.com. This means that when people want to visit your website, they will have to type in the name of your website followed by WordPress.com. This isn't actually the best way to create your website, because what you will find is that you are limited in terms of what you can do with it. For example, you are not able to install all the plug-ins and themes that you want; instead, you are restricted to the plug-ins and themes provided by WordPress.com. Also more importantly, with WordPress.com there is the possibility that your website can be taken down anytime without notice.

WordPress.org on the other hand is the place to be if you really want to utilize the full power of WordPress. Here you can download your own copy of WordPress absolutely free! You are then able to upload that copy of WordPress software on to your own web host. On WordPress.org, you can also download themes and plug-ins to install on your website. By installing your own WordPress onto your own web server, you have the freedom to install any plug-in or theme that you wish, or even have your own plug-in or theme created from scratch for your own custom use.

Why choose WordPress?

There are many open source content management systems around; they are all great tools, and each one has unique features and benefits. Furthermore, some people claim that WordPress is not up to the job, despite a number of high-profile companies who use WordPress to power their websites. So, why choose WordPress for your website? This is an important question for many future website owners ask themselves before they build a website. We will highlight just some of the reasons why choosing WordPress for your website is the best choice.

1. **WordPress is free**. Now, whenever you hear is the word "free", you might think that there is something wrong with the quality; but this could not be farther from the truth when it comes to WordPress. Actually, the fact that it's free makes WordPress simply the best Content Management system on the web. WordPress is not limited to a single team of developers; rather thousands of developers continuously improve WordPress with innovations that easily surpass the limitations of a commercial product. WordPress is a free and open source solution that has been created by thousands of competent, reliable and experienced developers. Every line of code has also been rigorously tested by millions of Wordpress users worldwide. WordPress gives you the ability to have a fully functional website. If you were to hire a developer to create your website it would cost you thousands of dollars and you would be tied in to a developer every time you wanted to make a change on your website. WordPress doesn't charge you when your website grows and hits a certain size, WordPress is perfect for organizations or individuals who are trying to save money on websites and can use that money to invest into other aspects of their business.

2. **WordPress is easy to use**. This is the number one reason that has made WordPress the most popular and arguably the best content management system on the Web. WordPress is easy to use; even senior citizens are able to use and set up WordPress websites in minutes. WordPress does not need a developer to remove outdated content on your website, make changes or even update the appearance of the site. WordPress has been embraced by the online community and has received such glowing praise and acceptance; this only proves that WordPress is the best CMS when it comes to user-friendliness.

3. **Easily customizable**. In a matter of minutes, you can have a very different look to your website, as WordPress utilizes themes to change the way your website looks. There are thousands of different themes available to apply to a Wordpress site, many of which are free, that allow you to change the look for your site. If you want a particular look, you can have a customized theme created to achieve the look that you want.

4. **WordPress is extendable.** WordPress is not limited to a simple blogging feature. If you want to create a particular website - for example, you want to sell products - then you can extend the functionality of your website through an e-commerce plug-in. Also, it is more than likely that the feature that you want to add to your website is available in the form of a plug-in and all you need to do is download and add to your WordPress website. You can download thousands of free WordPress plug-ins from **wordpress.org/plugins**. Furthermore, if the feature that you wish to add to your website is not available as a plug-in already, then you can hire developers to create a custom plug-in that will do exactly what you wish.

5. **WordPress is SEO friendly.** One of the main purposes for setting up a website is to receive visitors, and WordPress is extremely Search Engine Friendly (SEO). This means that search engines like Google will be able to index your website and enable users to find your content quickly and easily. In addition to having a content management system that is search engine friendly, you have several excellent SEO plug-ins that you can add to your website which will further increase your websites ranking in search engines.

6. **Solid support and foundation.** WordPress has been developed by thousands of excellent developers and it is robust enough for millions of users who use it for their online projects. Since WordPress is open source, this means that there are thousands of people who are constantly modifying, updating, creating themes, creating tutorials and plug-ins for WordPress and are working day and night to make WordPress even better. So, whatever support that you need, you are bound to find someone that will help you for free or at a very low cost. You are literally saving thousands! Because, if you hire developers to code a website for you from scratch, then you will have to pay for support in addition to the cost of development .

7. **WordPress is not platform dependent.** You can use WordPress whether you use Mac or PC. There are hundreds of hosting companies that will host your WordPress website and to my knowledge – I haven't come across a major web hosting company which is not able to host WordPress.

What kind of sites can you build with WordPress?

WordPress is more than just a blogging system; you can use WordPress to create almost any kind of site you want. Because WordPress is a content management system, you can use it to create a wide variety of websites and features that you didn't think were possible! Some people might try to dismiss WordPress as just a blogging CMS that is used by Internet marketers, but you will be surprised to know that even big brands use WordPress to run their websites. These include eBay, Yahoo, Ford, Coca Cola, Sony, Samsung, PlayStation, CNN, and the New York Times.

Coca Cola France

This is an example of how Coca Cola uses WordPress for its French website. You can have look at in more detail here: www.coca-cola.fr/

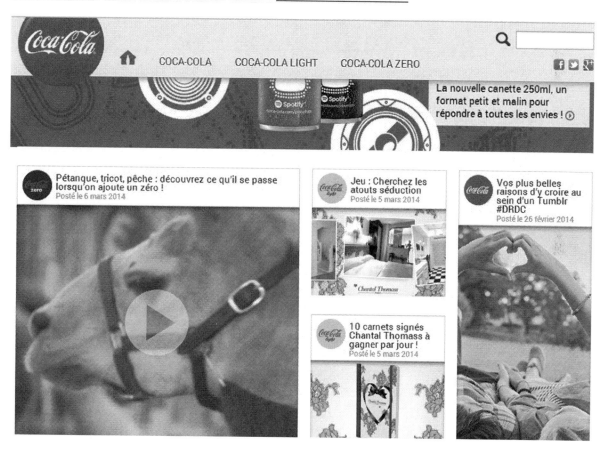

Sony Music

Sony music uses Wordpress for its official website. You can a have look at in more detail here: http://www.sonymusic.com/

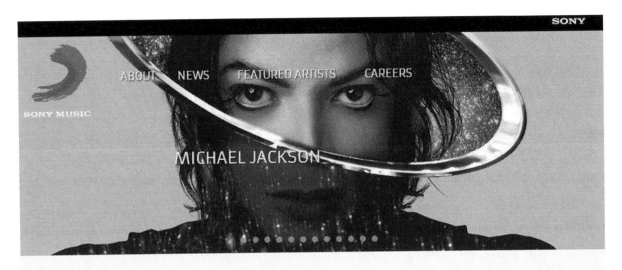

LABELS

  epic ARISTA NASHVILLE

The New York Times
NYT uses Wordpress for its corporate website. You can have look at in more detail here: http://www.nytco.com/

You can see a detailed list of some of the websites that use Wordpress on the official Wordpress showcase site here: http://wordpress.org/showcase/

How to find out if a website is using WordPress
Millions of websites use WordPress to power their sites, and in most cases it won't be apparent as the website owner will have customized the appearance. So if you want to find out if your favorite website uses WordPress, you could do a simple check by adding *wp-admin* to the website's URL. For example, if I wanted to find out if the Metro newspaper website in the UK uses WordPress, I would add *wp-admin* to the URL like this: *metro.co.uk/wp-admin* – if the website is using WordPress then you will be taken to the WordPress backend admin login screen.

What you will need

The best way to use WordPress is to have it installed on a web host account that you own, and this will enable you to really experience the full power of WordPress. WordPress has been created with the web scripting language called PHP and you will need a web host that supports PHP web scripting. Also, your web host will need to support MySQL which is the database that WordPress uses to store all of your content. The best thing about WordPress is that all of the major web hosting companies support PHP and MySQL; in fact, they have one click install software that will enable you to install WordPress in minutes. So, in order get your first WordPress website up and running you will need two things; a domain name and a web host.

A domain name

The first step that you need to take when you want to create a website is to choose a domain name. Think of your domain name as your website's home address. It is important to take your time on this step, as it will represent your brand. As a rule of thumb, you should choose a name that is short enough to remember and can get matching usernames for Twitter, YouTube and other social media platforms. There are many extensions available for your domain name such as .com, .net, .org, .info, .us, .biz, .tv and many more. The most popular and by far the best extension is the .com. To register a domain name, you do not have to be a company or an organization; anyone can register a domain name, and all you have to do is find a registrar (a company that manages the reservation of domain names) to register and buy a domain name of your choice. Here are some tips on choosing a domain name - please make sure you go through this before you register a domain name:

Your domain name should be your website name

This may seem obvious, but you'd be surprised to learn that not every website is named after the domain name. This is important for the simple reason that when people think of your website, they'll think of it by the name. This will help your users automatically know where to go, and they don't have to wonder what web address to type into their browser to get to your website.

Your domain name should match your brand name

The name that you use to advertise your product is the name that you want for your domain, because that's the first thing that people will type in their browser.

Get a short meaningful domain name

The key is to make sure that your domain name is meaningful and not obscure. You should avoid extremely long names, as people will not be able to remember your domain name; a long name will be a chore to type and trying to fit it as a title on your webpage will be a challenge.

Including "the", and "my" in your domain name

It is more than likely that the domain name you want to register has already been taken; in this case, the domain registrar (the company that you register your domain with) will suggest alternate forms of the name you typed. For example, if you wanted flower.com, and it was taken, it will suggest forms like; theflowers.com, myflowers.com. It will make the suggestions if they are not already taken as well. If you decide to add these forms to your domain, you should always remember to promote your site with the form of the name that you chose; otherwise, potential visitors are likely to forget to affix the necessary "the" or "my" to your domain name when typing it into their browser. There is a plethora of registrar companies to register your domain name with, each with its own features and benefits. But, the most reliable and arguably the cheapest registrar that you can use is NameCheap.com – a leading and genuine registrar which will let you register a domain for a bargain price compared to competitors.

Once you have decided on a domain name, you should register it right away before someone else does, or before the price of the domain name becomes too expensive. Go to www.namecheap.com create an account and register your domain name.

A web host

Next, you need web hosting for your website. Choosing a good web host for your website is one of the most important decisions you will take, because they are responsible for keeping your website online. If you have a poor web host, this will affect your website and you could potentially lose your whole site. The following are some key criteria that you should consider when choosing a web host:

Reliability and speed of access

The web hosts that you choose should be reliable and fast, and guarantee its uptime (the time when your website is functional). You should look for a minimum of time of 99%; in uptime terms this might actually be too low, and it should really be 99.9% or higher. If the web host company falls short of this reliability and speed then they should provide some sort of refund. Fortunately, there are some very good web hosts that have an uptime that is 99.9% or higher and have been known to be extremely reliable. For a list of the web host companies that I recommend you can go to www.expresstuts.com/wordpress-hosting.

Data transfer

This is sometimes called traffic or bandwidth. Data transfer concerns the amount of data that is transferred from the web server (rented from the web host company to hold your website files) to the visitors when they browse your website. Many web hosts advertise "unlimited bandwidth", but in actuality, the amount of bandwidth available to you is actually limited. Some web hosts will automatically suspend your website if it exceeds the amount of bandwidth that is allocated by the web host; otherwise, you will be billed for an exorbitant amount for exceeding the amount of bandwidth allowed.

Disk space

Just like bandwidth, many web hosts offer "unlimited disk space" web hosting packages. However, most websites will not use more than 100MB of web space. So, when you see web hosts offering packages with 100GB or unlimited space, be aware that you are unlikely to use that space, and it's important that you don't let a massive offer of disk space make you choose a particular web host company over other options.

Technical support

The nature of technology and your website's level of reliance on this technology mean that technical support is crucial to your online presence. The technical support department of a web host should function 24 hours a day, 7 days a week and this is often abbreviated as "24/7". You should not accept a web host that does not have staff working on weekends or public holidays, because it is possible that things will go wrong at the most inconvenient of times and it is important that you are able to get technical support when you need it most.

Make sure to avoid resellers

There are literally thousands of web hosts companies operating online, and you might see very cheap offers for web hosting. But, you should realize that not all web host companies own their web servers, which means that some of them are resellers for other host companies. The disadvantage of using a reseller is that you risk dealing with people who don't know much about the system that they are selling. It will take longer to get support when you have a problem because they will submit your technical support request to the actual hosting company for it to be resolved. Another disadvantage is that the reseller can go out of business; this will affect your website and you might find that your website suddenly and without warning no longer online.

When it comes to choosing a web host, you need to make sure that you complete due diligence and don't just jump at the first offer that you see. It is paramount your website remains safe and accessible at all times. I have compiled a list of the most reliable and trusted web hosts available here: www.expresstuts.com/wordpress-hosting - review the web hosts listed and choose a web host based on your needs.

Chapter 2: Getting Wordpress Up and Running

One of the features that make WordPress great is its ease of installation, WordPress is known for its ease of installation which is a very simple process and takes less than five minutes to complete. Many of the top web hosting companies on the web offer tools, like Fantastico and Quickinstall to automatically install WordPress for you.

The Famous 5 Minute Installation

QuickInstall

The 1-click install is the easiest and fastest way to install WordPress; most web hosts have a *cpanel* which is an interface where you manage your website files. The following screen shots will walk you through the installation process. Login to your cpanel, scroll down to the section where it says **Software/Services** and click on **QuickInstall**:

Once you click on Quick Install you will be taken to another screen where you can choose a set of software scripts that you wish to install. As we are going to be installing WordPress, we are going to select **WordPress** under the blog category on the left:

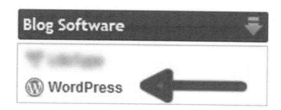

On the next screen you will be asked to confirm – just click on the **Continue** button to proceed with the installation:

You will then be taken to the final page before WordPress is installed on your server. Here you need to choose the domain that you wish to use WordPress with from the dropdown menu. If you only have one domain, that domain will be the one WordPress will be installed with:

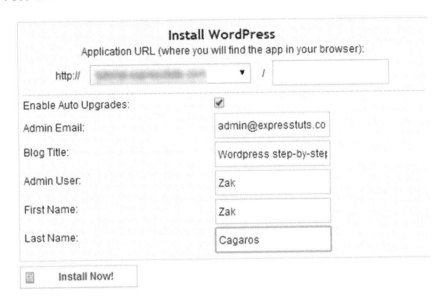

Be sure to leave the box next to the domain on the right empty, as we want to install WordPress in the root of our domain. You will need to enter the following:

1. **Admin email** – it is very important to enter this field, as this is where your password to log into the backend will be sent to.
2. **Blog Title** – This is the title for your blog, and it's the title that the visitors will see when they visit your website. Enter a title for your website - don't worry if you change your mind as you can change the title later on.
3. **Admin User** – here you need to enter the admin username that you will use to log into the administration back end of your WordPress website. Make sure you remember this username, as you will be using it to login to your site.
4. **First Name & Last Name** – enter your first name and last name here. WordPress will use these details to add to your profile as the site administrator.

Once you have filled in the form with the required details, just click on the **Install Now!** button and QuickInstall will install the WordPress script. Once the installation is complete, you will see a 'congratulations' message on the screen and you will be given a link to visit your blog:

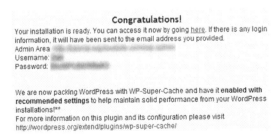

Finally, as part of the installation an email will be sent to the admin email that you provided which contains your log in credentials. These you need to log into the backend of your WordPress site.

Fantastico

Fantastico is one of the most popular script installation services that come bundled with most cpanel web hosting services. If the hosting company that you have chosen uses Fantastico, then the following will show you how to install WordPress easily and quickly using Fantastico. Login to your control panel and look for an icon that looks like this:

Alternatively, you can utilize the search facility available in all cpanel services. Just type in "Fantastico" and it will pull the icon up to the top of the screen. Once you have located the Fantasico icon just click on it and you will be taken to the next screen:

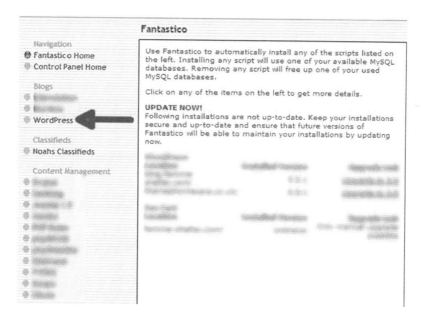

One the left hand side menu, you will see WordPress under the **Blogs** section. Simply click on WordPress, and then it will display the WordPress information screen:

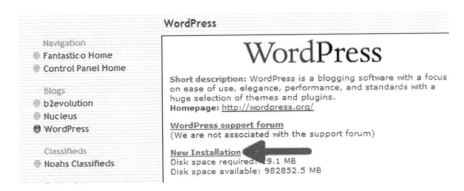

To install WordPress, click on the "New Installation" link. Next, you will need to select which domain you want to install WordPress on from the drop down menu. Again, we will leave the install directory blank because we want to install WordPress in the root of the directory. We want our website to appear as: mywebsite.com:

Similar to the QuickInstall process, you will need to enter some basic information including admin username, admin email and password, site name, description of your site and your admin nick name.

Once you have filled in all the fields on the form, just click on **Install WordPress**. You will be taken to another screen, there you will complete the installation by clicking on **Finish Installation**:

> **Install WordPress (2/3)**
> The MySQL database and MySQL user ▓▓▓▓▓_▓▓▓▓ will be created and used for this installation.
>
> - You chose to install in the main directory of the domain ▓▓▓▓▓▓▓▓▓▓▓.
> - The access URL will be: ▓▓▓▓▓▓▓▓▓▓▓▓▓▓.
>
> Click on **Finish installation** to continue.
>
> [Finish installation]

Make a note of your username, password, and the access URL that will take you to the website.

Chapter 3: Getting To Know Wordpress

The frontend as the user sees it

Now that you've completed the five minute installation of WordPress, it's time to take a quick tour of your WordPress website both in the front/public end and the back/admin end. Your new website is now installed and you should be able to view how the frontend looks like - just type in the domain of your website in the form of www.yourwesbite.com and you should see the frontend similar to this:

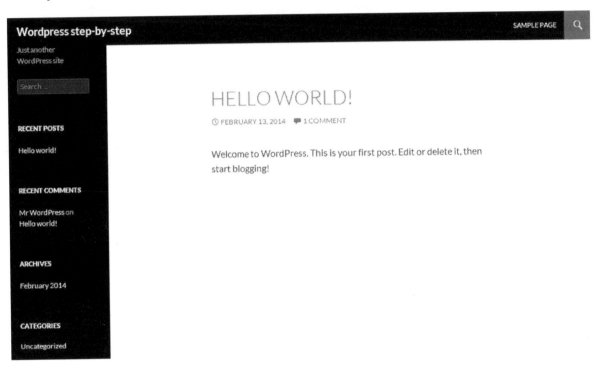

This is how the frontend of your website looks and you have successfully installed WordPress. Right now, there isn't much content on the website - only some of the pre-installed stuff that came with the WordPress installation. Next, we will be taking a tour of the backend of your WordPress website. This is where you will be pulling all the strings behind the scenes, and where all those WordPress websites admins control all those cool and exciting features that you have come to love and admire.

How to log into WordPress backend

To log into the administration side of your website you need to point your browser to: **yourwebsite.com/wp-admin**, where you will replace "yourwebsite" with your domain name. So, whatever your website's domain name you place "wp-admin" after your domain. You will then be taken to the log in page for your WordPress website:

Here you will login with the username and password that you chose when you were installing your WordPress. If you installed with QuickInstall, it will send an email with your password to the admin email address you provided at installation. So, go ahead and log into the admin end of your website.

How to change your password

The password generated on installation is usually quite complex. Unless you have a photographic memory, it is important to change it to something that you can remember. To do this you need to go to the **Users** section on admin backend and then click on **Your profile:**

Then scroll all the way to the bottom of the screen until you find where it says **About Yourself** and **Password.** Next, choose a new password by typing it into the New Password field. You will need to repeat the new password in the next field and then click on **Update Profile**. Your new password will be updated and you will get a message confirming that your profile has been updated:

Your workspace: The Dashboard

One of the fantastic features of WordPress is that it has two views - one is a public view where everyone on the web can see your website and another is the administration end, where only the admin (you) can access and view. This is where you control all aspects of your website and it's essentially the 'brain' behind your site. Once you've logged into the backend of your website, this is how it looks:

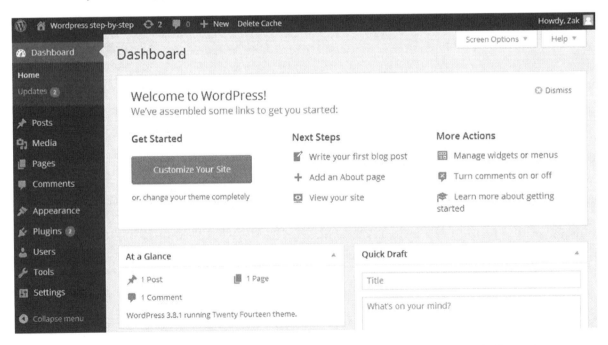

This is the headquarters where you will be in the driving seat and dictating every aspect of your website. Initially, when you log in for the first time you will see the middle main welcome box. That is a menu you can use to customize what you see - you can just click **Dismiss** on the top right corner of the message box. Now, everything that you see might look overwhelming to you, but don't fret - in no time you will be familiar with all aspects of the Dashboard. We will discuss some of the main elements of the Dashboard briefly, stating what each setting is used to control. The Dashboard side bar menu is where you can control different parts of your website. So, if you wanted to create a post, you would click on the **Posts** setting in the Dashboard and it would take you to the posts page where you can create, edit, and delete posts. Let us now briefly decode some of the control settings on the Dashboard:

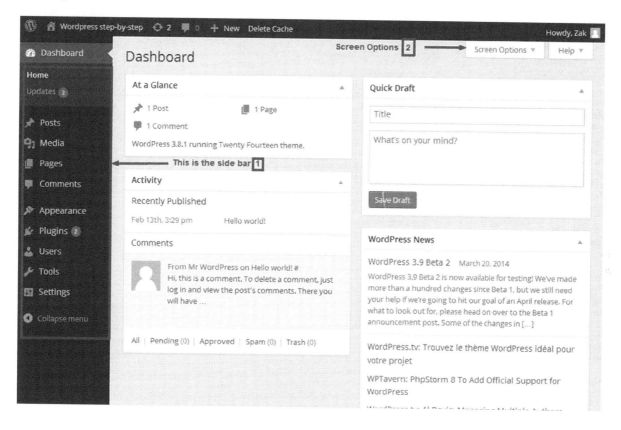

The Side Bar

The side bar contains the control settings for managing different aspects of your WordPress website. This is the area you will be using most of the time. Some of the controls in the side bar have sub-options that are not displayed by default so you need to hover over the menu item on the side bar and then you will see them. The controls in the side bar include:

1. Posts

Posts are the building blocks of what makes WordPress great - posts are essentially what make your blog what it is. Posts are the entries that are created by a blogger and are displayed in reverse chronological order on your home page. They have a comments field beneath which allows visitors to leave a comment on a particular post.

How to publish a new Post

There are two ways to create a new post from your Dashboard, but the easiest way is to use the Side Bar menu and click on the **Posts** tab and then Select **Add New**, like this:

You will then be taken to the **Add New Post** screen. Once here, all you have to do is fill in the blanks. Start by entering the post title in the upper field, and enter the content for your post in the body below the post title:

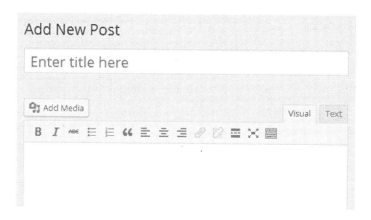

In the **Add New Post** screen you can choose further options before you publish your post, such as choosing a category to put this post under. You can choose multiple categories and you can put different posts under each category. We'll discuss categories in detail later, but for now just know you can create the post and select **Uncategorized**. When you are finished, just click on **Publish**. I will talk about Posts in much more detail later on. Create a quick post on your WordPress website following the steps outlined above. Don't worry too much about specific post details for now - just get your feet wet and make your first Post.

2. Media

Next up is the Media section on the Side Bar. Here is where you can make your website come alive by adding media content such as images, audio and video to your website. You can upload as much media content as you wish to your website and you can use this anywhere on your WordPress website. You can also upload media content while creating a post or a page. The Media control section allows you to edit, view, and delete any media that you have previously uploaded to your blog.

3. Pages

You have several options when you want to create content with your WordPress website - you can create posts, pages, or uploaded content in the form of images, audio and video. When you want to blog you will write a post, but when you want to create static content that is not arranged in reverse chronological order and content that does not change, you will create Pages instead. Pages are for content such as an "About", "Contact" or any other type of static content that you wish to display on your website.

How to publish a page

Make sure you are logged into the Admin section of your WordPress website. Then click on **Pages** and then select **Add New**:

You have a lot of flexibility in how you use pages in your website; you can have multiple pages and even subpages. You can use different templates for different pages on your website. We'll discuss pages in more detail later on, but for now just know that you can use pages for content that is static and doesn't change.

4. Comments

Comments are one of the pillars of the concept of blogging, as they enable visitors to contribute to your website by commenting on your posts or pages. If you ever wanted to know about your visitors' opinion on a certain topic, then you can utilize the comments feature in WordPress. When Comments are enabled for your posts and pages WordPress will display a form your users can use to respond to your content. The following is an example of a comment form:

![Leave a Reply comment form]

5. Appearance

The Appearance section is where you can change the way your whole website looks. Here you can control many aspects of your website, including:

- Themes
- Widgets (These are small blocks that perform a specific function)
- Menus
- Header
- Background
- Edit files

In the Appearance section you can change the theme of your WordPress site completely. Let's change the default theme that was pre-installed with WordPress. Make sure you are logged in, and then hover your mouse over **Appearance** in the side bar of your Dashboard and then select **Themes**:

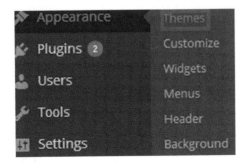

You will then be taken to the **Themes** page where you can change, install, and activate a new theme. Right now, the Twenty Fourteen Theme is active and we want to change it to another theme. We can either upload our own theme or install a theme directly from the free themes available at WordPress.org. For now, we're just going to change the theme to Twenty Twelve. To change themes, just hover over the Twenty Twelve theme and then click on **Activate**:

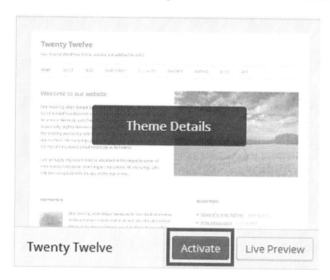

Once you have activated the Twenty Twelve Theme, hover over your site's title in the top left hand corner and then select **Visit Site**:

You have now changed the default theme; later on we will be uploading a theme and then activating it. We will also discuss the different sub menus available under **Appearance** in more detail later on. But, for now just know that the **Appearance** section in the Dashboard is a powerful tool within the WordPress arsenal that you can use to change the appearance of your website.

6. Plug-ins

Plug-ins are what make WordPress extendable. Plug-ins are small scripts that sit on top of your WordPress installation and they increase the functionality of your website. In other words, they let your WordPress website have more features and carry out additional functionality - such as a plug-in that will enable you to sell things straight from your website. There are thousands of free plug-ins available at the official WordPress.org site. You can check out the plethora of plug-ins available for you to add to your website here: www.wordpress.org/plugins. If you can't find a plug-in that does what you want, then you can simply pay a developer to create a custom plug-in just for your need.

7. Users

Gone are the days when the website was maintained by the computer geek, so that whenever an update was needed, the computer expert would go under the bonnet and make the necessary changes. With WordPress you can create additional authors and contributors to your website and in this section you can create an account for each author/contributor and set the appropriate permissions. This is a powerful feature, especially if you are going to have multiple contributors on your website like a blog magazine. The following is a breakdown of the different user roles and their permissions:

- **Administrator**: Has access to all the administration features - the super user!
- **Editor**: can publish and manage posts and moderate posts from other users.
- **Author**: Publishes and manages their own posts only
- **Contributor**: Are able to write and manage their posts but cannot publish them
- **Subscriber**: A user who can manage their profile

8. Tools

The tools section is a useful feature that you can use to export or import posts if you are moving from another blogging platform such as Tumblr or blogger to WordPress or vice versa.

9. Settings

The settings section is where you manage the settings for the whole website, and setup basic information for your website or blog such as the title, tagline, privacy settings and more. From here you can change your site's title and tagline; you can specify time zone & date format. You can also configure how you want your website to be displayed here - for example, if you want to have your home page as a static page, then you make those changes here. We will be looking at the settings section in more in just a moment.

Update notifications

From time to time you will see some numbers next to some of the menu items in the side bar. These icons are generated by WordPress to notify you when there's an update available for WordPress itself, a theme or a plug-in. Updates are an important part of your WordPress installation, because they often correct security vulnerabilities. Therefore, it is very important that you always update your site as soon as possible. So when you see a number inside a circle, then this means that there is an update available that you should install immediately. Updates take only a few seconds, and are crucial to keeping your website running smoothly and safely. To perform an update manually, click on the update icon in the toolbar - this is a circle made up of two arrows, as in the figure below:

There will be a number next to the two arrows that make a circle. On my WordPress website there are two. This indicates the number of updates that are available that you need to update and install.

Screen options

The screen options is a tab that is located on the top right corner in the backend of your WordPress site. You can manage settings related to the current page. The options that you get will depend on what screen you are in – just click on the dropdown arrow next to **Screen Options**, so if you're in the main Dashboard area then you will see the following options:

Here you can choose what you see when you are in the Dashboard. If you don't want to see WordPress news then just uncheck that box and this will remove the WordPress news box from the Dashboard. The screen options will change when you are in the edit post screen. As of this current WordPress installation you have the following options:

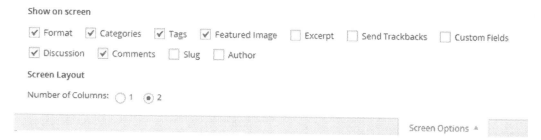

You can dictate what you see on the screen from here; so if you want to arrange the screen to just one column, then you can do so by selecting **1** from the number of columns. WordPress gives you tight control of what is displayed on your screen and how it is displayed.

Change basic settings

Now that you have had a brief introduction to the WordPress interface, it's time to make some basic changes in the WordPress settings section. We will make some basic settings in WordPress such as the site title & tagline, time zone, date & time format and we will tell WordPress which day the working week will start. To go to the settings menu make sure you are logged in and then hover your mouse over **Settings** menu and select **General** in the side on the Dashboard:

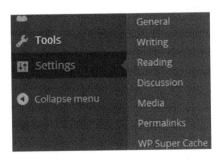

You will then be taken to the general settings page for your WordPress website, and from here you can set site-wide settings. In the settings page, customize your installation of WordPress by choosing a site title, tagline, admin email address (this is the email that you entered when installing WordPress - you can update if you need to) time zone and other settings that you wish to customize for your website. Once you are done, make sure to click on **Save Changes** to save your changes. Here is how my WordPress **Settings** page looks like after making changes:

General Settings

Site Title — Wordpress step-by-step

Tagline — WP The best CMS!
In a few words, explain what this site is about.

WordPress Address (URL) — http://tutorial

Site Address (URL) — http://tutorial
Enter the address here if you want your site homepage to be different from the directory you installed WordPress.

E-mail Address —
This address is used for admin purposes, like new user notification.

Membership — ☐ Anyone can register

New User Default Role — Subscriber

Timezone — UTC+0   UTC time is 2014-04-12 11:56:59
Choose a city in the same timezone as you.

Date Format —
- ⦿
- ○
- ○
- ○
- ○ Custom: F j, Y

Documentation on date and time formatting.

Time Format —
- ⦿ 11:56 am
- ○ 11:56 AM
- ○ 11:56
- ○ Custom: g:i a   11:56 am

Week Starts On — Monday

[Save Changes]

Writing Settings

The writing settings are found under **Settings** and from here you can control how WordPress displays formatting and publishing posts. WordPress will convert emoticons to graphics:

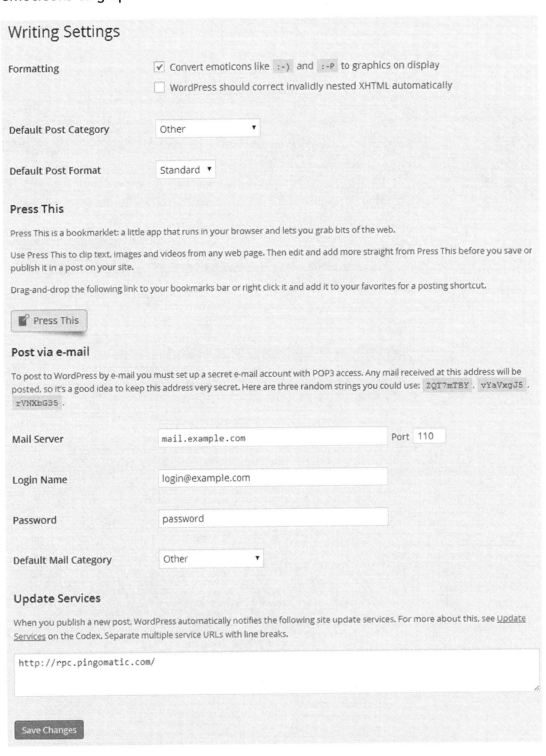

WordPress provides a **Press This bookmark** feature that helps you to blog about things you find on the web. This will help you to grab text, images and video from the web and post it to your blog. To use this feature, just drag the **Press This** link on this screen to your bookmarks bar in your browser. WordPress lets you blog from almost anywhere by using the **Post via email** feature; this allows you to send an email to your site with post content and this will be published from the email without having to log into your Dashboard. To use this feature, you will need to have access to a POP3 compatible mail server. The only limitation to this feature is that you can only post plain text with no special characters or HTML. The final setting in this section concerns update services. Whenever you publish a new post or make edits to your existing ones, WordPress will send a notification, known as a ping, to services to tell them about your new or updated post. This will help your blog to be discovered, and WordPress has pings setting enabled by default. The services that WordPress is set to notify is the rpc.pingomatic.com.

Reading Settings

Under the reading settings you can choose how you want WordPress to display on the front page of your blog. You have two options here under the **Front page displays option** - you can either have your latest post displayed on the front page or you can display a static page as the homepage:

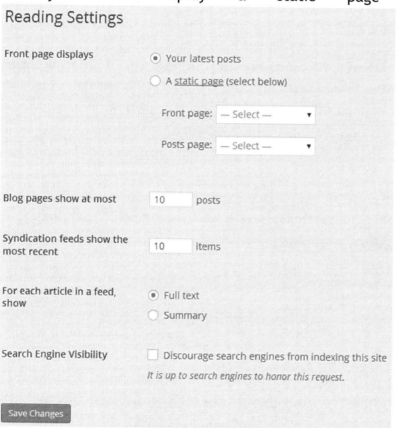

This will depend mainly on how you want to use WordPress. If you are going to have a lot of static content, then you might decide to use the static page as the front page; but if you are going to use WordPress for a news style website, then you will use the posts option as the front page. To use the latest posts option, just check the radio button next **to Your latest posts.** Or, if you want to use the static page option then check the static page radio button. If you decide to use the static page option, you can still create posts but you need to specify a designated page that will hold your posts. You can select which page you want to be the posts page under the **Posts page** option. You can only select the static page option if you have created pages on your WordPress website.

The next option is the **Blog pages show at most option**. This setting specifies the number of posts to be displayed per page on your site. The default number is 10, but you can change this to meet your own requirements. You might have more or less depending on how you want to display your content.

Syndication Feeds show the most recent option specifies the number of posts that readers will see when they download one of your site's feeds.

For each article in a feed, show – this option determines whether the feed will include the full article or just a summary. You can have the reader view the full text without a summary in the form of a snippet by checking the radio button next to **Full Text**; alternately, you can display a summary of your posts by checking the radio button next to **Summary**.

The final option in the reading settings is the **Search Engine Visibility** setting. You have the option to discourage search engines from indexing your site, and it has to be noted that this is not recommended, since one of the purposes of creating a site in the first place is to be found by readers, and they will most likely find your site and content via the search engines. Make sure to leave this option unchecked. To save all changes make sure to click the **Save Changes** button.

Discussion settings

The discussion settings page will let you set options for handling comments and publishing posts to your blog. This setting offers an extensive set of settings that you can configure, these include:

- Default article Settings
- Comment settings
- Avatars

Default article settings

This setting gives you three options for your posts, you will be notified whenever there are any external blogs lined to from the article, this is an important option, as you need to moderate what kind of sites that you want your site to be linked with. Make sure to check the **Attempt to notify any blogs linked to from the article** option to be notified whenever an external blog is linked to from your any of your posts. The next option under this setting is the option to allow link notification from other blogs, this will use the pingback and trackbacks feature. Let's first briefly understand what are pingbacks and trackbacks in the most non-technical way. One of the great features of Wordpress is the ability to leave comments on posts, and this can be very healthy for your blog. Pingbacks are a form of automated comment for a post, and this is created when another Wordpress blog links to the post. To further understand this, say you write a post on your blog, and someone else write a post on their blog and linking to your post. In your Wordpress site you will receive what is called a pingback, you will then be given the option to display the pingback as a comment on your post. Trackbacks are very similar to pingbacks, but the main difference is that it is manual and originates from an author of a blog. They would write a post on their blog and then send a trackback to your blog post so that their readers will be able to see their comment on the post. The majority of pingbacks and trackbacks are spam, or other bloggers that wish to get a backlink from your site. You should therefore disable pingbacks and trackbacks completely from your site. To do this make to uncheck the option that says Allow link notifications from other blogs (pingbacks and trackbacks):

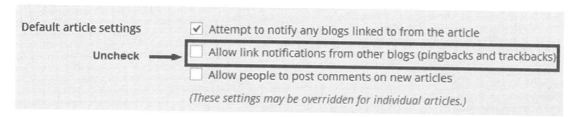

Comment settings

You have several options to configure when it comes to comments on your site; it is important to configure the comments settings properly when you first create a WordPress site, as you don't want to have spam or inappropriate comments left on your content:

You can specify who can comment and limit this to registered users only, although this will put off readers commenting because of the registration process, it will let you filter who can comment on your content. The most popular option for this is to only ask for the readers name and email when commenting on a post. You can close comments after a certain number of days. By default, WordPress closes the ability to comment on articles after 14 days. You can also specify how many nested comments you want to have - you should keep this number down for simplicity, as you don't want to have nested comments that are several levels deep. On popular blogs, you will see hundreds of comments on a post and these comments are broken down into pages with a certain number of comments shown per page. You can specify how many comments you want to show per page. You can also specify which comments will be displayed first. If you want to display the older comments first, which is the default setting, then you will select **Older** from the dropdown menu; or if you want to show the newest comments at the top, then select the **Newer** option. You also have the option to be notified by email whenever anyone posts a comment, or a comment is held for moderation. You can further control what comments appear by manually approving a comment.

Avatars

The final setting on the discussion settings page is the Avatars. Avatars are images that appear next to your name when you comment on avatar enabled sites. In WordPress, you can enable what kind of avatar you display for people who comment on your site. You have the option to disable this feature by unchecking **Show Avatars**. You can rate avatars based on content suitability. The default avatar for people who comment on your site is the mystery man.

Media settings

The media settings page lets you define settings for WordPress media uploads; the first option lets you set image sizes. When an image is uploaded, WordPress saves three instances of the image. You can adjust the sizes of the images from this page:

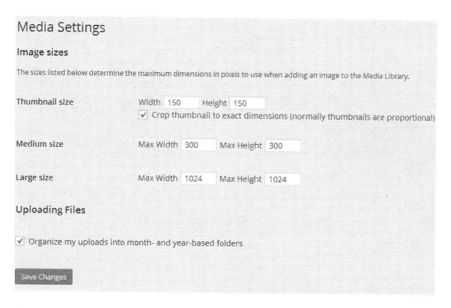

If an image does not fit the dimensions specified here, WordPress will crop the images down to size. The second option lets you organize your uploads by month and year and groups these into folders.

Permalinks

Permalinks are the URL links that WordPress generates when you create posts and pages on your site. By default, the links created by WordPress have question marks and many numbers and this makes them very unfriendly to humans and search engine bots. Since this is an important topic, we cover permalinks in detail in chapter 4. Go through each of the settings mentioned here, and make sure to set all of the recommended settings.

Remove sample content

When you installed WordPress, it automatically installed some sample content to fill your new website. This includes a "Hello World" post, a comment and a sample page. Before we create our own content to fill the website, we need to first remove this sample content.

Delete the "Hello World" Post

We will start by deleting the sample post "Hello World", and to do this you need to be logged into the WordPress admin backend. On the side bar menu hover your mouse of over **Posts** and select **All Posts**:

You will then be taken to the All Posts screen. This is where you manage, create, edit and delete posts. The only post that is published on your website now is the sample post. To remove a post, just hover your mouse cursor over the title and menu will appear below the post title, from the menu, you can edit, trash (delete), and view a particular post:

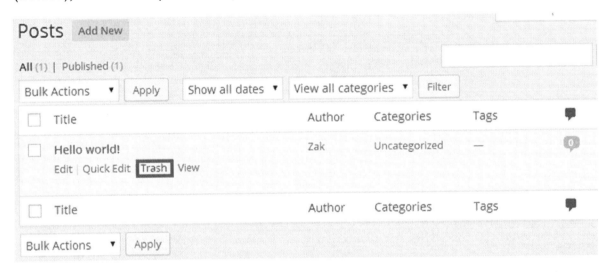

To delete this post just click on **Trash** and it will be removed from your published posts. By deleting a post, WordPress will automatically delete any comments associated with that post. Also, in the event that you delete a post in error, or you wish to restore a post that you have previously deleted, you can do so by going to the Trash bin section in your WordPress website. This was not available previously as we have never deleted anything since installing WordPress. But now that you have deleted the post, you will find that a Trash icon has appeared in the Posts screen with the number of items in the trash in brackets - we've only deleted one item so there is only one in between the brackets:

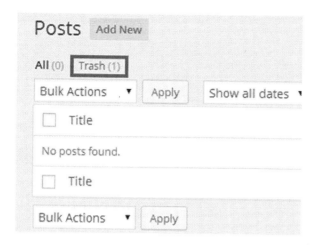

To view all trash items and to restore a post, just click on Trash and you will be taken to the Trash section of your posts. To restore or permanently delete any trashed item, just hover over the title and a menu will appear:

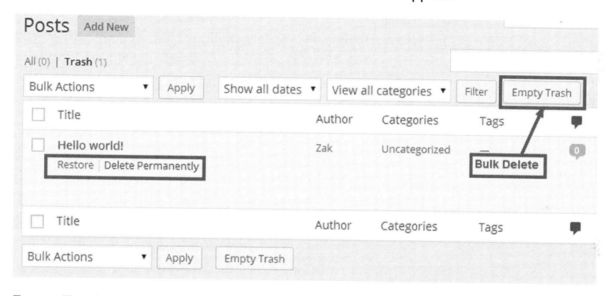

Empty Trash lets you delete multiple items permanently from the trash.

Delete sample page

The next step is to delete the sample page that was part of the WordPress installation. This was installed to show you how a page looks like on a WordPress website. To delete the sample page, you need to hover your mouse cursor over **Pages** on the side bar menu and select **All Pages**:

Like the **Posts** screen you will be taken to the **Pages** screen where you can create, edit and delete pages:

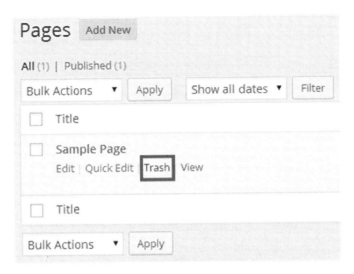

You can delete the sample page in exactly the same manner as you deleted the posts previously - just hover your mouse over the page title and select trash from the menu that appears beneath the page title. Similarly, you can restore and permanently delete pages by clicking on the **Trash** icon that appears when you delete the page. This process is the same as deleting or restoring a post - you can restore, delete permanently or delete multiple items permanently from this screen. .

Remove Widgets

WordPress also configures some widgets automatically after installation; this is all done so that your website has some content that you can customize. First, what are widgets? Widgets are small blocks within your WordPress website that perform a specific function. They add content features to your side bar and examples include a search box, list of your links on your website, and categories. WordPress gives you a list of widgets that you can drag and drop on your side bar, and the best part is that you are not limited to what WordPress offers. You can have a custom widget on your side bar for any particular function that you want. Typically, WordPress configures the following widgets on your side bar: Search, Recent Comments, Archives, Categories, and Meta. This is how they look on the front end of your website:

We will delete all but one of the widgets on the side bar; we will keep the search widget as this is useful for enabling visitors to search your website. To delete the widgets from the side bar, make sure that you are logged into the admin backend, then move your mouse over **Appearance** and then select widgets:

You will then be taken to the widgets screen; this is where you configure which widgets that you want displayed on your side bar:

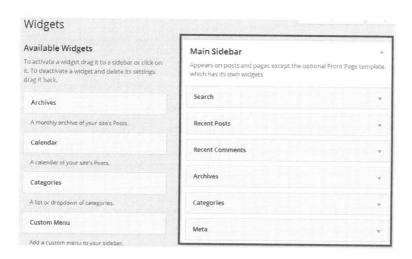

In the Widgets section, you have two columns - on the left, you have the **Available Widgets** and on the right, you have the **Main Side Bar** and the widgets that are currently displayed on the frontend. When you want to add a widget, all you have to do is drag and drop the widget of your choice from the left column and place it inside the **Main Side Bar**. For now, we want to delete all but the search widget. To do this, just click on the drop down arrow next to each widget and the widget will expand to reveal a title box and the delete icon to remove the widget from the Main Side bar, as follows:

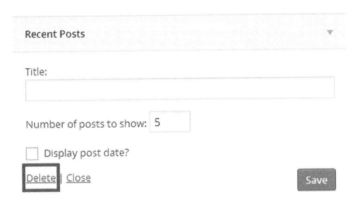

To remove the widget from the side bar, just click on **Delete** and the widget will be removed. Once you have deleted the widgets, you should only have the search widget left on the side bar in the frontend:

Plan your site

Creating a WordPress website is not just about installation, creating content, adding images and everything else in between. You need to have an overall plan for your website, whether you are creating a personal blog or a web business. With WordPress you can create beautiful and functional websites, but the success of your website will largely depend on the thoughts you put into it before you build it. Therefore, it is important to have a plan if you want to be successful with your website. You should ask yourself some basic questions that will help create a direction for your website - the following are 3 basic questions that you could ask yourself and will help you to create a solid plan:

1. Why are you building a website? When you create your website, it should serve a purpose. This could be a personal blog where you share your views on a particular topic, or a sales website. Knowing your site's purpose will help you determine what features and functions the site will have.

2. Who is your prime audience? In other words, who are your customers and what are their demographics? How old are they? Do they have interest in your topic? What percentage is male or female? Are they educated? When you know your audience, it will help you to write content that engages them and they will respond by sharing your content with friends and family. It is very important to know who your audience is, because if you don't know who you're talking to it is difficult to know what to write. It could mean that you go in the wrong direction which will waste e your time, money and resources – it will not result in a viable end product.

3. What do you want your visitors to do? This is another important question to consider before you create your website. It is directly linked to the first question. So, if your goal is to drive online sales, then you want your visitors to make purchases; or if you are creating a website which is specific to a niche and you want to make recommendations as an affiliate, then you want your visitors to use your affiliate links to buy products and services.

Once you are armed with this crucial information, you'll be able to sketch out your basic site structure - these consisting of the pages you want on your site, how they will be linked together and what content to put on the homepage, etc. This will help you immensely when you sit down to create content for your website. It is important to take time out briefly before you create your website to create a plan and understand what kind of website you want to create and what you want to get from your site. Using the questions outlined above, create a simple plan for your website. This doesn't have to be a thesis, even one page with three paragraphs that answers the questions we discussed will be enough.

Tuesday

Chapter 4: Creating Killer Content

How to Create Posts

Creating engaging content is to websites what food is to humans; a website is nothing without content, as the saying on the internet goes, "content is king". At the heart of WordPress websites are Posts and they are one of the primary sources of content for your website. Creating posts will become an important part of your daily tasks that you do as an administrator, and once you master the simple art of creating posts you will be well on your way to populating your site with engaging, quality content. We briefly looked at how to create a Post earlier; we will now look at the different parts of a post in more detail.

To add a Post you have two options - you can click on **New** icon next to the plus sign in the tool bar at the top:

Or you could go to the first menu item in the side bar which is **Posts** by hovering your mouse over **Posts** and then selecting **Add New**:

Either way it will take you to the **Add new posts** screen where you can add a new post. As we're going to be using this quite a lot, let's familiarize ourselves with it:

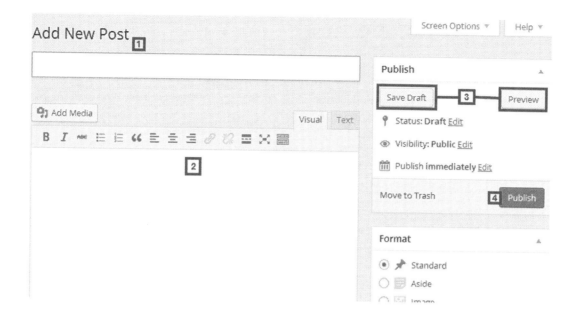

1. Post Title. The first thing that you need to do is give your post a title and this is where you will enter the title for your post. The post title is very important, as your visitors will see your post title before seeing the content in the post, so make sure that you title your posts appropriately.

2. Post Content. The all-important content of your post goes in the main body area, and you can add text, audio and video as part of your post. To make sure that your post is formatted properly, make sure to use paragraphs to split up your text. This will ensure that your text is not too crowded and the user is able to see a nice readable format of your text. You can use the toolbar to format your text further; the toolbar has all the formatting functions that you need such as bold, italic, number list, bullet points and alignment. This gives you a greater control of format to present your text within the post.

3. Save & Preview Buttons. You can use the **Save** button to save a draft copy of your post and the **Preview** button lets you preview your post before you publish and make it live on your website.

4. Publish button. You will no doubt be pressing this button all the time - you will hit the **Publish** button when your post is ready and you want to publish your content to the world! When you successfully publish a post, a yellow message box will appear at the top of the page that confirms your post has been successfully published. Now that you have familiarized yourself with the post screen, it's time to put what you just learned into action and create a post.

How to show part of a post as a preview

I'm sure you've seen articles that show you the first few lines as a preview and have a small link next to the last sentence to go to the full article. This is an effective way for displaying several different articles to your readers and they can choose which article that they wish to read in detail without being shown the full text. You can do this easily and quickly from the formatting toolbar when you are creating your post - there is an icon with two bold blocks and dashed lines in between. When you hover your mouse over, it will say "**Insert More Tag**":

You can use this feature to split up the text of your post and only show a preview to the reader. To insert the "more" tag, place your cursor after the paragraph that you want to show as the preview and click the **Insert More Tag** icon from the formatting toolbar. It will display a long rectangle box that has the text "more" inside:

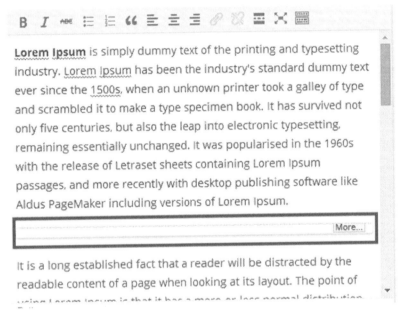

Once you have added the "more" tag, click on the **Update** button, and your post will now only show a preview of the full post with a link to go to the full article:

Example Post #1

Lorem Ipsum is simply dummy text of the printing and typesetting industry. Lorem Ipsum has been the industry's standard dummy text ever since the 1500s, when an unknown printer took a galley of type and scrambled it to make a type specimen book. It has survived not only five centuries, but also the leap into electronic typesetting, remaining essentially unchanged. It was popularised in the 1960s with the release of Letraset sheets containing Lorem Ipsum passages, and more recently with desktop publishing software like Aldus PageMaker including versions of Lorem Ipsum. Continue reading →

How to Create a Sticky Post

WordPress was originally created for blogging, but has now matured into a platform that you can use to create almost any kind of website. One feature that is embedded into the WordPress DNA is the ordering of posts by date, with the most recent post occupying the top spot. This is usually fine, but at times you might want to create an important post that you want to feature at the top of the list, and not go down as soon as you publish more posts. Sticky posts are useful in displaying important information that you want your readers to read. For this you will need what's called a sticky post. You would create a sticky post exactly the same way you create a normal post but you activate a feature that will make your post stay at the top of all posts. When you are creating or editing a post, you can designate a post as sticky simply by clicking on **Edit** next to where it says: **Visibility: Public** on the right hand side and you will get a small sub menu. From here, just check the box next to **Stick this post to the front page**:

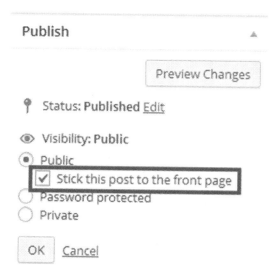

Your post will now show at the top of all posts. If you wish to remove this post as a sticky post, you can simply uncheck the box and WordPress will remove it as a sticky post and arrange it according to date. If you have more than one sticky post, WordPress will display the most recent sticky post first.

Updating a post

WordPress has become the platform for creating your website, and not only because it is easy to use but it lets you update your content easily. Beginners to blogging and WordPress believe that once you write a post then that's it, you can't make changes or update it. The beautiful thing about WordPress posts is that you can update any post any time. In fact, this is very important, because you might have new information that is useful to a post that you created months ago.

To edit a post that you have already created, go to the backend and to the posts screen. You will see a link to edit the post when you hover over the title of the post. Click **Edit** and you will be taken to the Edit Post screen. This is the same as when you create a new post; the only difference is that the button on the right is now **Update** and no longer **Publish**.

Post publishing options: Delayed publishing

WordPress has so many great features and the scheduled publishing feature is definitely one of them. You might not always publish your posts straight away, and you might want to wait a little while before putting it on the web and making it live. This could be for many different reasons; maybe you want to coincide with a particular event or launch of a product or you want to publish your post at a particular time or day of the week. Delayed publishing allows you to specify a future publication time - this gives you a timeframe for you to return to edit your post or even cancel it together. Once you set the time to publish the posts, you simply save everything and your posts will be published when the time arrives and not a second before!

Like everything else with WordPress, scheduling a post is very straight forward. To schedule a post, just follow these simple steps:

1. Make sure that the time settings match your time zone. If WordPress is configured with a different time zone to yours, it's likely that the post won't appear at the time you've scheduled it for. So, to make sure that the time settings are correct, just go back to the **Side bar menu** in the **Dashboard** and click on **Settings** section and then select **General** and set the time according to your time zone, if not already set.

2. Write your posts as you would normally by choosing **Posts** and then select **Add New** in the Dashboard. You will then be taken to the **Add New Post** screen.

3. Once you have written the content for your post, click on the **Edit** link in the **Publish** box on the right and a new group of settings will open:

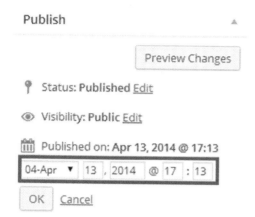

You can set the time and date that you wish to publish your post down to the minute. When you are done, just click **OK** to apply changes and the **Publish** button will change to **Schedule**. To complete the post scheduling process, click on **Schedule**. You can change the time by simply editing the post.

Categories: Organizing Your Content

WordPress makes organizing your website easy with Categories and Tags. When you create a post on your WordPress site, you can file that post under a category that you specify. A category is like a folder that describes the topic of a group of posts. For example, if you had a website on movie reviews, you could have a post on the Terminator 2 Movie and this would be filed under category Sci-Fi. You can name categories according to what kind of posts will go under it. So, in our movie review example we could have several different categories such as Romance, Action, Crime, Thriller etc. All good WordPress sites have categories that arrange the posts and make them easier to find when browsing. When you create a post, you have the option to assign that post to a category. If you don't assign a post to a category, WordPress automatically selects the **Uncategorized** category which is a default category from the WordPress installation. This is considered bad practice when running a website on WordPress. In order to always give the impression that you are running a professional website, you must have appropriately named categories that you can place your posts under. Therefore, you should rename your Uncategorized category to something more appropriate such as 'Other', 'Miscellaneous or' 'Random'.

When starting out with your website, it's not always necessary to create all of your categories at once. Since you will be creating content regularly, you can create categories on the fly based on the topic that your posts will be talking about. You can have as many or as less categories as you want, but this will largely depend on the different kinds of the things your posts will be dissecting.

How to create a category

Creating categories is a simple process in WordPress. In the Dashboard hover your cursor over **Posts** from the side bar menu and then select Categories:

You will then be taken to the Categories page - here you can create, edit and delete categories:

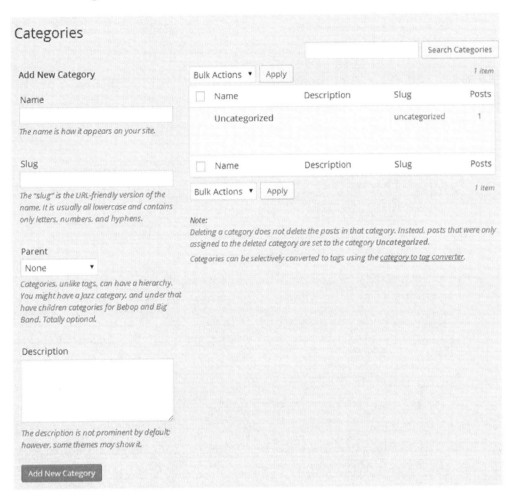

To create a new category, just type in the name of the category you wish to create where it says name, then type in the Slug which is the URL friendly version of the category name. This is usually the same name but in all lowercase. You can specify a parent category, in which case the category will become a subcategory of the parent category. You can also add a description of the category in the description box. When you are finished, just click on the **Add New Category** button and your category will be created. We mentioned that it is good practice to rename the uncategorized category to something more appropriate. You can do so by hovering over the **Uncategorized** category and selecting **Edit.** You will then be taken to the Edit Category page where you can rename the category. You can also add categories right from the Add New Post or edit Post page - you can do this by clicking on the **+Add New Category** link right at the bottom of the categories box:

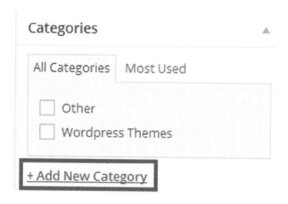

Now that you've seen how easy it is to create and edit categories, it's time for you to create your first category and rename the Uncategorized category to something more meaningful such as 'Other'.

How to assign a post to a category

Once you have created categories that will hold your posts, you can easily assign a post to a category when you create one or you can edit a post and assign it to a category by selecting the category from the list of categories available in the Edit Post page. When adding a new post, you are given the option to assign that post to category in the Categories box which is on the right:

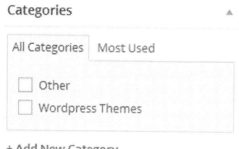

To assign the post to a category, just click on the checkbox next to the category that you wish to add the post to and click on **Publish** button if you're creating new category or **Update** if you're editing. The categories box has two tabs, **All Categories** and **Most Used**. If you have many categories, WordPress makes it easy for you to choose your category from the most used tab, which displays the categories you frequently use. If you haven't done so already, make sure to assign all of your posts to an appropriate category, otherwise if you forget, WordPress will assign it to the default category - the Uncategorized category - if you haven't changed the name already.

Tags

Just like categories, tags sort and organize your content to improve the usability of your site. This helps readers to browse through your site content by topic rather than browse your content in a chronological way. While categories are the broad groupings of your posts, tags are there to describe specific details about your posts. You can think of tags as your site's index words and you can use them to further categorize your content. The tags that you use will always be dependent on what your post is all about. Let's say you have a personal blog and you have the following categories: Food, Travel, Movies, and Books. When you want to write a post about that delicious pasta you had at an Italian restaurant, you will assign the post to the Food category first and then you can add appropriate tags such as Pasta Bolognese, Pizza, Steak, etc.

How to add Tags to your posts

Just like creating categories, adding tags is also a very simple process. When you create a post, you can create tags and add it to the post or you can add tags to an existing post via the Edit Post Page. Either way, look for a Tags box, which is located just under the Categories:

Tags

[ ] Add

Separate tags with commas

Choose from the most used tags

You can add a tag several ways - by typing the tag into the text box, and then clicking the **Add** button; or you can type all of your tags at once into the text box. Separate each tag with a comma and then choose a tag for your post. You don't have to write tags for all of your posts, as you can re-use tags that you have already created by clicking on the **Choose from the most used tags** link. Tags are there to collate your related posts together, and it is important that you don't get too carried away with the process. Here are some guidelines on using tags:

1. Limit the number of tags. In WordPress, you can assign as many tags as you want to a post, but it makes good practice to limit your tags to no more than 10. Only add more than 10 tags per post if you feel it is necessary.

2. Re-use the same tags. You can reuse the same tags on different posts when it is appropriate, and if your website is about a particular topic, then chances are that you will be able to re-use most of your tags since they will be related to the same subject.

Using Clean URLs

When you create a post WordPress will automatically assign it a URL link within your website's content, so that the post can be easily found and linked to within your site. Readers will access your posts in several ways - they can access the posts by visiting your front page; browse through the posts and categories. Another way that readers will find your content is through the search engines when they perform a search for a particular word phrase and this is the most likely way that readers will find your content on the web. By default, WordPress creates URL's that are not search engine friendly in the form of "http://site/?p=id. ID". This URL identifies the post number, so your first post will be p=1 and the number will change depending on what post number is displayed. This is not user friendly, as you don't know what each post is about; all that is displayed is the post ID and we don't know what that post's title is and what it's about.

When you install WordPress, one of the first things that you should do is to change what's called the permalinks. Permalinks are the permanent URLs that WordPress assigns to your posts, and this is the link that readers and bloggers will use to link to your article. Search engines are not able to properly rank your site's content if you're using the default permalinks, because they need to know what your posts are about so that they can rank them on search results, which will help your site to be found by visitors. WordPress is truly optimized for Search Engines and you can change the permalinks to user and search engine friendly descriptive URLs that search engines can find easily. To change the URL structure on your site, you need to hover your mouse over **Settings** in the Dashboard and then choose **Permalinks**:

You will then be taken to the Permalink settings page where you can set how WordPress generates URLs for your posts:

Common Settings

○ Default 1   http://tutorial.expresstuts.com/?p=123

○ Day and name 2   http://tutorial.expresstuts.com/2014/04/19/sample-post

○ Month and name 3   http://tutorial.expresstuts.com/2014/04/sample-post/

○ Numeric 4   http://tutorial.expresstuts.com/archives/123

◉ Post name 5   http://tutorial.expresstuts.com/sample-post/

○ Custom Structure 6 http://tutorial.expresstuts.com
                       /%postname%/

1. Default. This is the default setting for permalinks. This uses the post ID and is neither search engine nor user friendly.

2. Day and name. This options includes generating permalinks based on date and name, options include; the year, month, and date separated by slashes. With this option, WordPress appends the description of the post name in a simplified format. E.g. *WordPress.org/2014/01/17/name-of-the-post-simplified.*

3. Month and name. This is the same as the day and name, but the only difference is that it leaves out the date number. E.g. *WordPress.org/2014/01/name-of-the-post-simplified*

4. Numeric. This option is similar to the default setting, but it doesn't use the characters "?p=" in the URL. It appends the text /archives. E.g. *WordPress.org/archives/post-number*

5. Post name. This option takes out all of the date information, and only uses the post name. e.g. *WordPress.org/name-of-post* this creates not only user friendly URLs but more importantly search engine friendly URLs. When permalinks include numbers, these make no sense to humans and search engines but WordPress uses them to find and store data in the database. This permalink structure is the most accurate when it comes to describing your content and this is important for both search engines and human visitors.

6. Custom structure. If you have specific requirement for your URL link structure then you can use this option. With this option, you can tell WordPress exactly how

it should generate permalinks. This is ideal if you want the post category to appear in the permalink. you can use this option to include the category in the permalink and it would look something like this: /*%category%/%postname%/*.

Permalinks have become an important part of search engine optimization techniques and using Post name option will help your posts to be found by the search engines. Once you have selected Post name, just click on **Save Changes** to apply the setting universally. WordPress will update any posts already published that are not following this structure, so you don't need to manually make changes to posts that have been configured with the default permalink. Be sure to set the permalink settings early, because if you make the change after making several posts, then any users that bookmarked these with the old structure will find that they can no longer access the post.

Long post titles

When you select the Post name option, WordPress generates a URL based on the title of the post. This sometimes means that you have long URLs and may even include special characters. You can tweak the URL of a post while creating it or when you edit a post. Inside the Add New Post or Edit page, you can manually change the URL permalink of a post. The permalink of the post appears directly under the post title text box, and you can just click on the Edit button to shorten or remove special characters from the URL:

When you click on edit , you can simply edit the permalink either by shortening it by removing certain words or special characters. Once you have finished editing the permalink just click to save your changes:

Pages

WordPress is not just about Posts that are organized by the date they are published; this might have been the case several years ago, where WordPress was considered only a blogging platform. If you don't want to have dynamic content where users can interact with the publisher, then you can use pages to present static content that doesn't change. The most frequently questions that first beginners ask is what's the difference between Pages and Posts?

Pages v Posts

The question of whether to use pages or posts has been asked thousands of times before, and no doubt will be asked many times again in the future. As you have seen already, posts are content that is organized in reverse chronological order, this means that the newest posts will be displayed at the top of the page and the oldest posts go to the bottom. Posts are organized in terms of the date that they were written. Users can interact with your content by commenting on a post - this is one of the standout features of WordPress. Pages on the other hand are static content that doesn't change and is not organized by date; rather, pages are organized in a hierarchy. Pages are useful when you have content that you want to present on your site and keep it there permanently. An example would be an "About Me" page, where you provide biographical information about yourself. If you did this in the form of a post, it would eventually be pushed right down the list as you publish more and more posts. Therefore, in this case you need to use a page to keep that information at the forefront of your website. Another use for pages is a frequently asked questions page, where you display a list of all of the common questions and their answers. It would not be appropriate to use a post to display this kind of content, as it will get lost in the sea of posts that you have and users will have to browse through your posts to find it. Pages are static content that users read to get informed, and you wouldn't want them commenting on an About page, for example. But, it is worth noting that this is a feature available in WordPress and if you don't want comments on the page, you need to disable this feature so that readers do not comment on your pages.

There are many important and essential uses for pages in WordPress. If don't want to have a blog, but you want to have simple site that displays content only , then you would use pages for this purpose. Simple sites that present static content with pages are very much different to posts as the element of interactivity with the content is not present with pages. Millions of WordPress websites utilize both posts and pages. One example of this is when small businesses use WordPress to create the static content as pages such as information about the company, policies, products and services. They can then use the posts and the blog feature for latest news and promotion. The following table summarizes the key differences between pages and posts:

Pages	Posts
Posts are organized by date	Pages are not organized by date
Posts are social, they allow users to interact by allowing comments	Pages are not social; users don't interact with a page like an "About me" page.
Posts are categorized based on topics	Pages are not categorized, but are hierarchical.
Posts become outdated and are archived	Pages are timeless and do not expire

How to create pages

Now that you now the differences between a post and a page in WordPress, let us see how you can create a page. You can create pages pretty much the same way you create posts. In the WordPress backend Dashboard, hover your mouse over **Pages** and then select **Add New**:

As you did previously, you will be taken to the Add New Page screen:

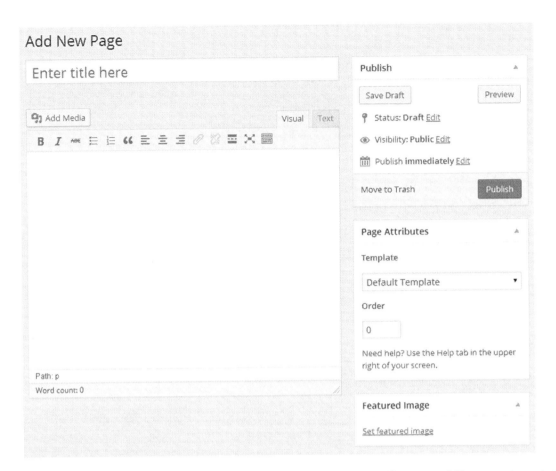

The parameters for adding a new page are very similar to adding posts; at the top, you specify the title for your page. You have a main body where you can add content, just like when creating posts. You have the option to use the visual editor or the HTML view. You have the publish box on in the top right - here you can tweak settings and again you are able to schedule your page, but this is not something that you would do often. You can also further refine your page by using page templates from the page attributes box - here you can choose what kind of page that you want to use. Depending on the theme that you have installed, you will have different options to use for different pages - for example, if your theme has a contact template, then you can use this template when creating a "Contact" page for your site. With pages, you can also set a featured image. This is an optional feature and you don't have to always set a feature image, but highly recommended. Once you are finished creating your pages, just click the **Publish** button to create the page. This is how our page looks:

Sample page #1

Lorem Ipsum is simply dummy text of the printing and typesetting industry. Lorem Ipsum has been the industry's standard dummy text ever since the 1500s, when an unknown printer took a galley of type and scrambled it to make a type specimen book. It has survived not only five centuries, but also the leap into electronic typesetting, remaining essentially unchanged. It was popularised in the 1960s with the release of Letraset sheets containing Lorem Ipsum passages, and more recently with desktop publishing software like Aldus PageMaker including versions of Lorem Ipsum.

It is a long established fact that a reader will be distracted by the readable content of a page when looking at its layout. The point of using Lorem Ipsum is that it has a more-or-less normal distribution of letters, as opposed to using 'Content here, content here', making it look like readable English. Many desktop publishing packages and web page editors now use Lorem Ipsum as their default model text, and a search for 'lorem ipsum' will uncover many web sites still in their infancy. Various versions have evolved over the years, sometimes by accident, sometimes on purpose (injected humour and the like).

Pages are another way WordPress lets you present your content. Now that you've seen how to create a page, it's now time for you to create a page and include a featured image.

Comments

Comments are the lifeblood of blogs on the web, as comments let you connect with your users directly. Commenting lets your users feel that they are connecting with you and you can also use comments to promote yourself and get backlinks from popular websites to your site. You can gauge how popular a website is just by looking at the number of comments that it has on its posts; readers will notice the number of comments that a site attracts to its posts and this will attract readers to visit your site and read the most popular posts. The more popular your site becomes, the more comments you are likely to get. This also brings with it the unwanted comment type, which is spam. At some point in your sites lifecycle, it will experience spam, and this is likely to come from comments.

In this chapter we'll look at the WordPress comment system - how to enable, moderate, and leave a comment. As a site administrator, you can get bogged down by the mundane tasks of filtering and moderating comments on your site, so we'll also look at ways to identify spam and a plug-in that you can use to help moderate spam.

Moderating comments

By default, WordPress settings enable comments on your site and this is evident when you see a "Leave a reply" section at the bottom of posts and pages. Comments are more suited to posts than they are to pages, as the pages contain static content such as location and biographical details. WordPress gives you so much flexibility to deploy and manage comments. It is highly recommended to enable comments on your site, as this will not only help your site to be noticed, but also make it more interactive and entice users to come back. We've already looked at how to configure moderating comments briefly in the settings section of WordPress. Under **Discussion** settings, WordPress gives you fine control on how comments are filtered. You can disable comments on individual posts, and this will override the universal setting to allow comments. One setting to make sure that you disable is the pingback and trackback setting. This feature has been known to bring lots of spam, and content plagiarism.

You can enable or disable comments when you are creating or editing a post. Inside the post, click on **Screen Option** in the top right hand corner of the screen just under the toolbar, and a menu will drop down. Make sure that Discussion is ticked:

☑ Discussion

This option will display the discussion box when creating or editing a post. If it isn't expanded just click on the down pointing arrow and it will expand to reveal discussion options for the post:

Discussion

☑ Allow comments.
☐ Allow trackbacks and pingbacks on this page.

Here you can set whether you want to allow or disable commenting for a post. As explained previously, make sure that the checkbox next to trackbacks and pingbacks is not checked. If you want to disable comments entirely, you can do so from the **Discussion** settings page and this will be applied to the whole site.

How to leave a comment

Commenting on relevant blogs and posts can help you promote yourself and your site online. If you configured WordPress to ask for only a name and email address, this will allow users to comment quickly and easily. To see how the commenting feature looks for your site, you need to be logged out and access your site's URL as if you are a normal visitor. Browse to one of your posts, and you should see "Leave a Reply" at the bottom of your post:

Leave a Reply

Your email address will not be published. Required fields are marked *

Name *

Email *

Website

Comment

You may use these HTML tags and attributes: `<a href="" title=""> <abbr title=""> <acronym title=""> <b> <blockquote cite=""> <cite> <code> <del datetime=""> <em> <i> <q cite=""> <strike> <strong>`

[Post Comment]

To leave a comment, WordPress needs a name and an email address. You also have the option to give your website's URL in the Website box; this will help create backlinks to your site. In the comment box, you can use HTML tags to format your comments further. This means that you can use bold, italic and underline formatting features. We're going to leave a comment on our post, so that we can better understand the commenting process. Make sure to fill out all of the required fields - i.e. the name and email, and include a comment. Once you click on **Post Comment**, you will see your comment appear under the post:

Zak
April 24   at 3:11 pm

Your comment is awaiting moderation.
A great blog yo have here. I'll make sure to visit regularly. Keep up the hard work.

Reply ↓

But this doesn't mean that your comment has been approved; just above your comment, it tells you that your comment is awaiting moderation and hasn't been approved yet. This is how your comment will look once it's moderated and approved but for now, only you can see this comment as you are the one has written it. Now let's log back into the WordPress admin Dashboard and see how to moderate a comment. As soon as you log into the Dashboard, you will see a number in a circle next to the **Comment** menu on the side bar:

This means that you have a comment and is awaiting your moderation. To moderate the comment, just click on **Comments** and you will be taken to the Comments page. From here, you can approve, mark as a spam, delete and even edit comments:

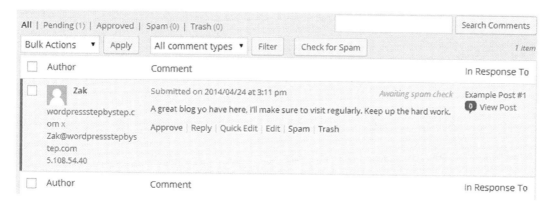

To moderate a comment, hover over the comment text and you will be presented with a menu to either approve or delete the comment. In our case, we will edit the comment first, as there is a letter missing in the word "you" and then we will approve the comment. To do this, just click on **Approve**, and the comment will be approved and should now appear under the post on the frontend of WordPress:

The comment is now live, and anyone who reads the post will be able to see the comment. WordPress makes it easy for you to moderate comments, and when your readership grows, you will no doubt have many comments on your posts. You can moderate comments right from your Dashboard without having to go inside the Comments page. To do this, click on **Screen Options** in the top right hand corner and make sure that the Activity box is checked. WordPress will then display an activity box in your Dashboard and from here, you have links to your recent activities and you can moderate comments without needing to go inside the comments page:

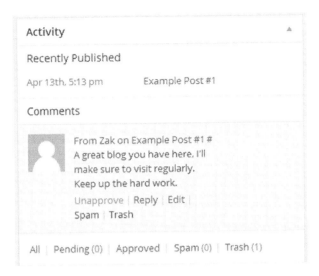

Preventing comment spam

Nothing is more frustrating than receiving unwanted spam, as if those emails trying to sell you Viagra weren't enough. Spam is nothing new; since WordPress sites allow commenting, and as the site grows in popularity, it will become a target for spam bots. The first step in combating spam is to make sure that WordPress doesn't automatically approve comments. To do this, go to the Discussion settings page on the Dashboard and make sure to check the box that will hold comments for moderation:

If you don't turn this setting on, WordPress will automatically approve all comments submitted and this could mean that all spam comments will be accepted, and you could have a host of comments full of pornography, Viagra, and other spam links. The next step is to activate the pre-installed anti-spam plug-in – Akismet. The Akismet plug-in does a great job in catching those spam comments and deleting them before they even reach your moderation tray. To activate Akismet just go to the plug-in page by clicking on Plugins and you will see a large button at the top of the screen that says Activate your Akismet account:

When you click through to the activate button, WordPress will give you an option to enter a key or to get a key for free by signing up. Just click on Get Your API key and you will be taken to the Akismet's registration page. Sign up for an account by entering the requested details. Akismet is free for personal use, so just select the personal option and click **Sign up**. The Akismet website then takes you to a payment page - don't worry, this is optional and they want you to make a donation. Since we're going to use it for personal use, just move the slider to Zero and then click on continue. Finally, you will be presented with a key. Copy this key and save it somewhere on your computer. Go back to the Akismet page on WordPress and then paste the key into the box provided and then click **Use this key**:

You will then be presented with a final page to save your account details:

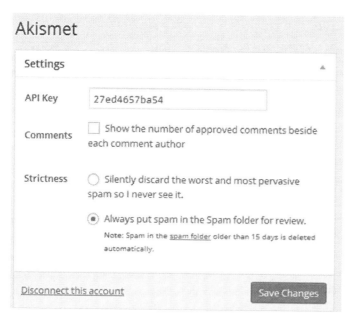

Before you save all changes, select the final option on how spam comments are filtered. Always put spam in the Spam folder for review; this option will let you review all the comments that have been marked as spam. Since Akismet is not perfect, it will sometimes mark legitimate comments as spam, and this will enable you to approve genuine comments from the spam folder. To finalize everything just click on **Save Changes**.

Avatar

Engaging in discussion with someone on your website is very different to talking to someone in real life. But, you still want to experience that person's uniqueness, and WordPress lets you do this by personalizing comments with an avatar. An avatar is a small image next a person's comments and is usually a picture of the person that made the comment; but this can also be something else that the user chooses, such as a cartoon image. An avatar helps you to visually identify the person that left a comment in a conversation and it gives you a visual image of the person. WordPress supports avatars, but you can't add an image from inside your site. You can get an avatar image from your Facebook or Twitter accounts, or you can use WordPress' very own Gravatar service. Gravatar stands for Globally Recognized Avatar and is an online service that provides users with free avatar images that can be linked to their emails. Whenever you make a comment on a WordPress powered site with this email, WordPress will pull your personalized avatar from its online Gravatar service.

Getting a Gravatar image is straight forward - go to www.Gravatar.com and sign up with the email that you use most often to comment with. Once you have created an account, you can add an image and then choose a rating for your Gravatar, which is a measure of the picture's suitability. You have four options to choose from when rating your Gravatar - G – a Gravatar with this rating is suitable to be displayed on all websites with any audience type; PG – this rating contains rude gestures or provocatively dressed individuals; R – this rating suggests that the image contains harsh profanity, nudity or violence; X – the final and most extreme rating suggests that it contains hardcore sexual imagery or extremely disturbing violence. Most WordPress websites only display Gravatars that have a G rating, and this can be changed from the **Discussion** settings page.

Chapter 5: Creating an Attractive Website With Themes

When you set out to create a website, you have a picture in your head about the way you want your site to look. WordPress lets you dictate to the smallest detail how you want your site to look and as you saw already, WordPress is flexible enough to look exactly how you want it to. The only limitation is your imagination here! In a matter of minutes, WordPress lets you install a different theme, and gives your site a fresh look. There are thousands of themes available on the web both premium and free, and if none of these meet your standards, you can have a theme created especially for your site from scratch. A WordPress theme is a set of files that control how WordPress arranges and styles your content. All WordPress sites start out with a standard default theme that is pre-installed when you deploy WordPress for the first time. Depending on the version of WordPress you're running, this will be called different names. You can use the default WordPress themes and you can customize a theme to your site but you can get another free or premium theme, or have one made for you from scratch. The most popular option is to use themes that have already been created, whether free or premium. There are thousands of themes available, from real estate to animal care themes; you have an extensive choice. The ease of installing and changing appearance is one if the main features that make WordPress the best CMS platform on the web.

Install custom header for your theme

One of the first things that a visitor who comes to your site will see is the header area on the front page of your site. The header area is at the top of your homepage, and it is important that you create a homepage that looks as professional as possible. The current theme does not have a custom header and this makes the site look unprofessional. We have the twenty twelve theme activated, and we have chosen this theme because of its nice, simple layout which doesn't have too many colors. By default, the theme does not have a custom header, and we need to install a custom header that matches our sites motto. To change the header, hover your mouse cursor over **Appearances** and then select **Header**:

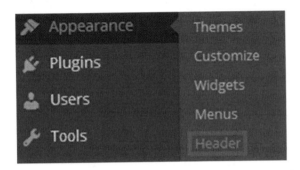

You will then be taken to the Custom Header page where you can upload a custom header for the theme. The suggested width for the header is 960 pixels width and 250 pixels height. If your have an image that is bigger than the suggested width, you will be given the option to crop. We have already created a header that meets the suggested size of 960 x 250 pixels, and we can upload our header by clicking on **Choose File** and then we will browse for the image on our computer:

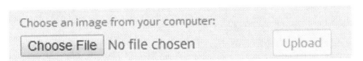

Browse for the image file on your computer and click **Upload**. You will be given the option to crop your header before it is installed on the theme, since the size is the same as the recommended dimensions we will go ahead and click on **Skip Cropping**, Publish Image as is. Once you have finalized your header you will be shown a preview of how it looks and there will be a message that says your header has been updated:

Before you save all changes, make sure to uncheck option **Show header text with your image**, as this will overwrite text on your header image. Click **Save Changes** and then visit the frontend to see how your header looks:

By removing the header text from the header, we created a header that looks more professional and pleasing to the eye. If you don't want to have a header, you can simply remove it from inside the custom header page where you uploaded the header. Just scroll down until you can see the button **Remove Header Image**. Once you have uploaded a header, image it will be available for you to use again even if you remove it.

Customize theme background

WordPress gives you more options to further customize the theme; you can customize the theme's background. You have two options to configure the themes background - you can either upload a background image or change the background color. You can use an image as the background and the image will be repeated from top to bottom and left to right. The second option is to change the background color, and this is the most common setting used when configuring the background. You can tweak the colors of the theme background to blend with your header image. The background color in the twenty twelve theme is visible only on the top and bottom of the theme. Some themes will have the background only on the sides and others will all the way round. To change the background color, just click on Background under Appearance, and you will be taken to the Custom Background page:

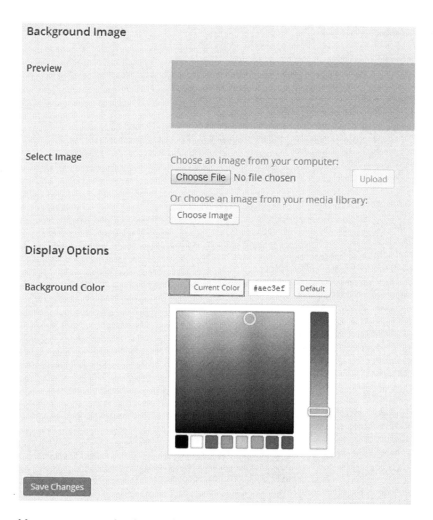

You can tweak the colors and make a blend that matches your header color, once you have found the perfect color just click **Save Changes** to apply your new background color and then visit the frontend of your site to see how it looks.

Customization menu

WordPress provides a separate customization menu that contains all of the settings that you will need to fully customize your theme. To get to the customization theme, just click on **Customize under Appearance** and you will be taken to the Customize screen, where you will be shown a preview of how your site looks on the frontend. You can make changes and these will appear in the preview in real time and let you see how your site will look as you make changes before you save:

You are given several options to customize your site on the left, and you can click through each setting one at a time to customize. These options have been put here under customization, but you can find each setting separately in the Dashboard. For example, you can get to the background setting through the background link under appearance, and you can get to the site title and tagline under the settings menu in general settings. All of these settings have been put here under customization, so that you can easily customize your site from one place without having to go into different sections on the Dashboard.

The theme editor

If you want absolute fine control of all aspects of your theme, then you can use the Theme Editor under appearance to edit the theme under the hood. This is for advanced users only, but if you are confident with code, then you can go straight into the core code of the theme and make detailed changes to the theme from here.

How to download and install a new theme

With the power of themes, you can spice up the appearance of your site in a matter of minutes, and there are literally thousands of themes for you to choose from. Our first stop will be the official WordPress.org themes section and you can download and install themes whilst inside the WordPress Dashboard. You have two options to download a theme - you can either download the theme from the official themes page at http://WordPress.org/themes, or any other website, then upload and activate; or you can download the theme directly from the Appearance and Themes menu and activate without uploading. Whichever method you choose, downloading and activating a theme will only take you a few minutes. We'll download and activate a theme from inside the Appearance menu in the

Dashboard. In the Dashboard, hover your mouse over **Appearance** and then select **Themes**:

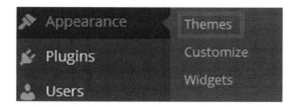

The themes page will open and this is where you can upload, install and activate themes, currently we have three themes installed and Twenty Twelve theme is activated. To install and activate a new theme just click on the **Add New** button or you can click on the plus sign:

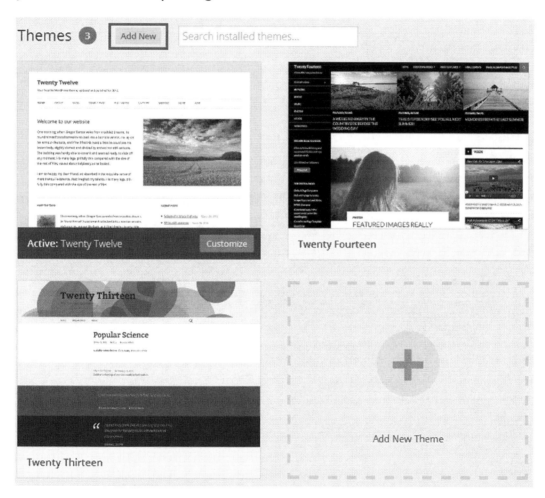

Both options will take you to the Install Themes page, and it is here where you can upload, install and activate a new theme:

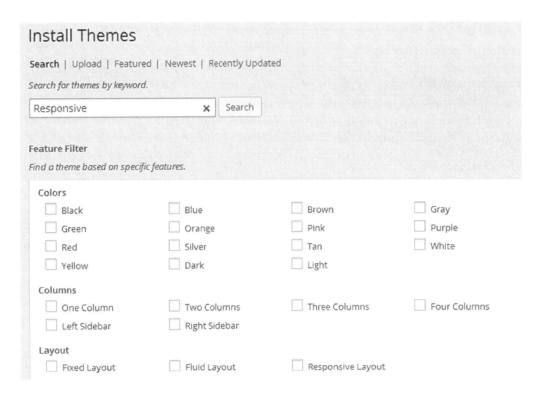

Since our theme is in the official WordPress themes directory, just type in **Responsive** in the search box and it will be the first theme. You can also do an advanced search for a theme in the themes directory; you can specify the colors, columns, layout, features, and even by topic. We already know what theme we want to install, so we just search for it quickly:

Click on **Install Now** to install the theme on your site. WordPress will then begin unpacking the files and installing the theme; this should be immediate and you should receive a message that says theme has been successfully installed. You have now installed the theme onto your site, but it hasn't been activated which means that it is not currently set as the theme for your site:

You can preview the theme to see how it looks before you activate it and make it live. To activate the theme, just click on **Activate**. Have a look at the front end of your WordPress site to see how your new theme looks. You can do this by either typing in the name of your site into a new tab on your browser or you can hover your mouse over you sites name and then select **View Site** as follows:

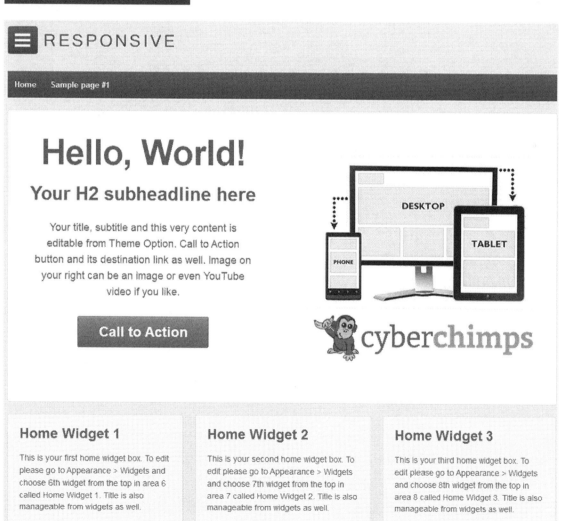

The theme that we installed comes with some sample content that shows you how you can use the theme. WordPress separates the content and the appearance, so this means that all of our content is still intact and the only thing that has changed is the theme. We will now customize some features of this theme to our website; the theme comes with an extra set of menu options that will enable you to customize the theme easily. Hover your mouse over **Appearance** once more and then select **Theme Options**, the themes options page will open as follows:

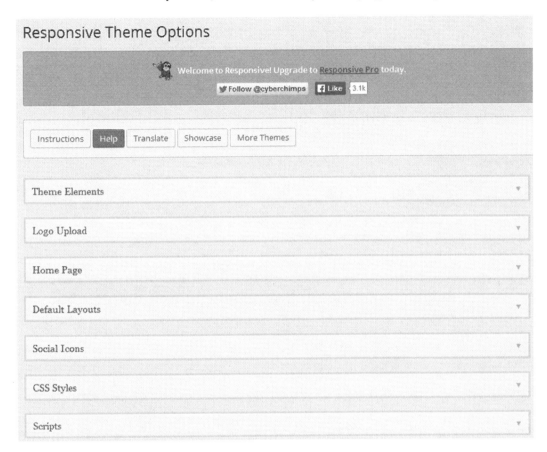

From here, you can customize your theme further and you are given several options to do this. We will start with the homepage, so click on the drop down arrow next to the homepage:

Make sure to uncheck **Override the WordPress frontpage option**, as we want to display our blog as the home page. If you like, you can use this option to have a static homepage and you can place your content on the content area inside the Home Page menu. Click **Save Options** near the bottom and the homepage should now display your posts instead of the static homepage.

Free themes v Premium themes

Themes are probably one of the most important parts of a WordPress site, since it governs how your website looks. There are thousands of free WordPress themes available online, and this gives you a wide choice of themes. When first starting out with your site, one of the first decisions that you have to make is whether to use a free or premium theme. Using a free theme makes sense because why should you pay for a theme, when you can get one for free? There is no straight forward answer to this question but hopefully the following factors might convince you to change your mind:

1. **There is no support and updates with free themes.** These two things are crucial to your site because WordPress is always improving and moving forward. The theme that you use also needs to be updated to take advantage of new features. With free themes, there usually is no support. That means that should you run into problems, there is no one to turn to for help. There is one exception to this, which is that if you are well versed in the dynamics of how themes work and you are able to create, edit and update themes, then you could use free themes, and update them yourself.

2. **Most free themes are not SEO friendly.** Search Engine Optimization has become a necessity in today's online landscape. Premium themes have been created with SEO and they are usually created with a solid framework such as the genesis and thesis frameworks.

3. **Features.** It's no longer just about a good looking theme anymore; the features that come with a theme are just as important. With free themes the features offered is limited, and again as we highlighted before there is no support available to implement any of the features that are available.

4. **Encrypted themes.** There is now an increasing trend among free theme developers to encrypt their themes. Theme encryption takes place when the developer of a theme prevents a user from removing footer links that link back to the developer's website by hard coding the links into the theme. Some of these links could be advertising products and services that have no connection to the website, and users get frustrated.

Using a free theme is something that 90% of new WordPress users will use, but as their website grows, they will need more features and support to customize the theme. In terms of cost, premium themes prices range from anything between $35 to $80.

Widgets

As you've already seen, widgets are small blocks on your WordPress site that perform specific functions. Widgets appear on the sidebar either on the left or right side of all WordPress sites. Widgets are very useful as they enhance your site by offering your visitors a host of different kinds of content. Widgets work with all WordPress themes, which means that even if you change your theme your widgets will still work; you might just change their positioning on the page based on the new theme. When you first install WordPress, you have some widgets that appear on the sidebar. These include - Recent Posts, Archives, Categories, Recent Comments, Meta, and the Search widget. Earlier, we removed all but the search widget, and we will now configure some widgets and put them on the side bar.

Widget settings

Widgets enhance WordPress sites by offering additional content in the form of block sized boxes; visitors find them very useful as they are able to navigate the sea of content on a site by using the widgets on the sidebar. You can setup widgets very easily. In fact, all you have to do is drag and drop and your widgets are ready to go. As with everything about WordPress, it offers you even more options to further customize and refine widgets. All of the widgets in WordPress have settings that can be adjusted, and you can configure the settings of any widget by clicking on the down-pointing arrow in the right corner. To demonstrate this we'll configure the Recent Posts Widget. You can get to the widgets section from the Dashboard by going to **Appearance** and then select **Widgets**:

This will take you to the Widgets page. Right now, we only have one widget in the side bar and that's the Search widget. From the Widgets page, you can activate a widget by dragging it to the sidebar. To delete and remove a widget, you can drag it back to the left side under the Available widgets area:

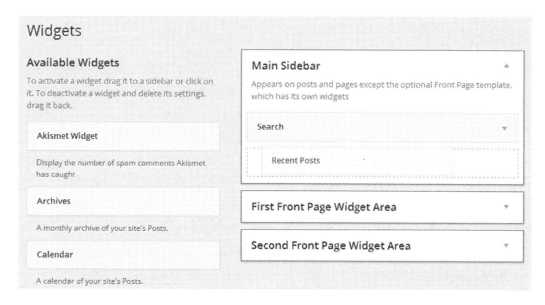

You can also dictate the order of the widgets. If you want the recent posts to be the first widget then you just drag it up and the rest of the widgets will move down. Once you decide where you want to put it just drop the widget and it will fall into the side bar neatly. To go into the settings of a widget, just click on the arrow pointing down and it will open up the mini settings menu inside the widget:

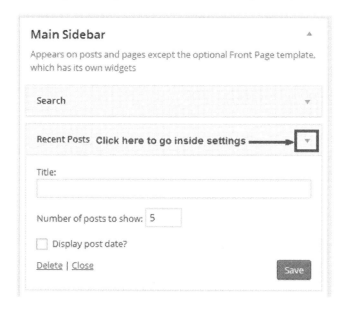

The settings for each widget will be different - the Recent Posts widget gives you the option to configure the number of Posts that you want to show and if you want to show the date of each post. A couple of settings that all widgets will have is Delete and the Title. If you no longer want to use a widget on the side bar, you can either drag it back or click on **Delete** to remove it from the side bar. All widgets will include a title box, which you can use to give the widget a custom title; this means that you can rename the Recent Posts widget to "New!" If you want to keep the default name for the widget you can leave the title box empty and WordPress will use the widget's default name. WordPress gives you the option to remove widgets but keep their settings; this is useful for when you need to remove a widget temporarily and you want to add it back without losing the original settings. There is an inactive area on the widget page right at the bottom under the available widgets area. You can drag and drop the widget here and WordPress will remove them from your sidebar but keep the settings of each widget:

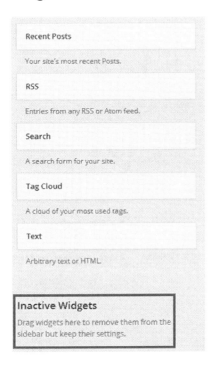

Then, when you want to add the widget back to the sidebar, you simply drag and drop it back without configuring the settings as they are already saved from before.

Core widgets

Widgets add superb functionality to your WordPress site and WordPress gives you so the many options to customize and even add your own custom widget with the Text widget. There are core widgets that WordPress provides for you, and it's important that we understand each widget and its functionality.

Categories

The categories widget shows your visitors links to the different categories that you have on your site. Users can browse the different categories and they can go straight to a particular category that they may be interested in without having to search extensively. You can configure the categories widget to show posts as a dropdown or show post counts and hierarchy. These options depend on the amount of content that you have on your site and as we've just started out, we may not be able to fully utilize this feature yet.

Custom Menu
As if you didn't have enough options with the menu system, WordPress gives you more options to create a widget that contains a custom menu of pages that are on your site.

Links
All good websites have links and as your site grows, it will have links pointing to both internal and external targets. The Links widget lets you display a group of links that point to other content.

Pages
If you have extensive content on your site, you can use the Pages widget to display links to additional content in the form of static pages.

Recent Comments & Recent Posts
This is a neat Widget, as it shows the most recent comments left on any of your posts. Users will be able see and read the most popular posts just by looking at the number of comments each post has. The Recent Posts widget lets your visitors see the new content that you have published on your site without having to browse through posts and categories.

Search
An important feature that every website should have is the ability to search through your site's content from a search box. This is neatly provided via the Search widget, your visitors can search your content quickly.

Text
The Text widget provides the most options when it comes to widgets, as it can be used to create a custom widget for anything that you want. The text widget accepts HTML, and this means that you can embed custom code inside the text widget. If you want to add a custom Google search box or a video from YouTube, you can do this easily with the text widget.

Help your visitors find what they want: Creating Menus

When you create pages, they are not always displayed on the frontend of your site and you have to create links to the pages that you create. The twenty twelve theme that we are using automatically adds any pages that we create to the default Menu that was already configured when you installed the theme. It is important to note that other themes do not have this feature and you have to manually create a menu and then add pages and links to it. This gives you more control and you can specify exactly where you want to place your menus, what pages to add etc. WordPress has a whole section dedicated to menus in the Dashboard. Hover your mouse over **Appearance** and then select **Menus**:

This will take you to the menu settings page for the theme that you currently have activated; in our case, it's the twenty twelve theme:

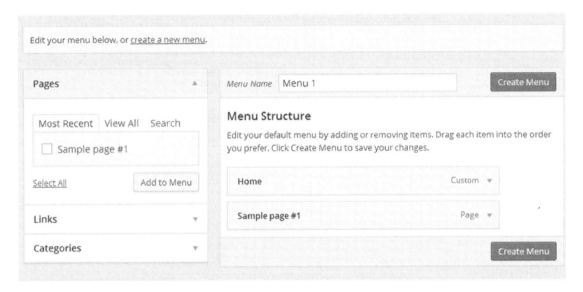

Here is where you manage the menus that appear on your site. You can add multiple menus on your site; some themes have a location for a primary menu and a secondary menu on the frontend. WordPress gives you the option to put pages under another page and make it a subpage. To do this, you would drag the page that you want to make a subpage slightly to the right and it will be indented as follows - this means that the page is now a subpage or child page of the page above it:

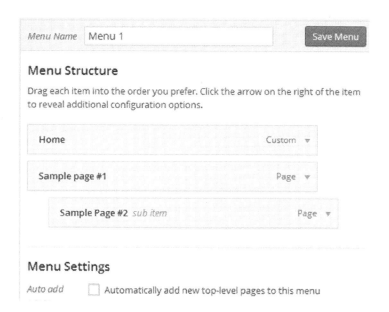

Click on **Save Menu** to save all changes. Now let's see how the menu is displayed on the frontend of our site:

Wordpress step-by-step

Just another WordPress site

HOME   **SAMPLE PAGE #1**

SAMPLE PAGE #2

The second page has now become a child of the first page and is displayed as a drop down menu. WordPress gave us a simple drag option, whereas before you would have to write the code to get the same result.

Instead of using the default menu that WordPress created, you can create your own custom menu and use this instead. To create your own custom menu, just click on create a new menu link that appears just under the two tabs:

Give your menu a name and then click on **Create Menu**:

Once you save all of your changes, you can now select your menu from the list of available menus from the dropdown box:

You now have a brand new menu, but you haven't added any items yet. To do this, just select the checkbox next to the pages that you want to add to your menu in the pages section and then click on **Add to Menu**:

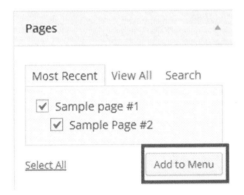

When you have added the pages to the menu, they will appear under the Menu Structure. This is where you can arrange your menus. As we saw earlier, you can make a page a subpage or the child page of another page by dragging it slightly to the right.

Add Links and Categories to Menu

You can add links and categories to the menu. For example, if you wanted to link to a page on another website, you can do this easily by clicking on Links and then specifying the URL of the page that you wish to link and the link text that will be displayed as the menu item in the frontend:

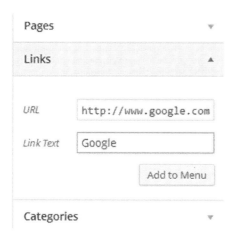

Once you have added the URL and the link text, just click on **Add to Menu** and your link will be added to the custom Menu you created. Again, you can manipulate how you want to display the link menu the same that you can make a page a child page of another page. The Menu section also lets you specify where you want to place your menu on your site; this will be different depending on the theme that you are using. Different themes will have different locations to place your primary and secondary menu items on the frontend of your site.

Wednesday

Chapter 6: Getting More Out of Your Site With Wordpress Plugins

WordPress is packed full of features that lets you create a great looking website in minutes. To really experience the power of WordPress, you need to install essential plug-ins that will increase your site's functionality. As of this writing, there are over 30,000 plug-ins available in the official WordPress plug-ins directory. This is a staggering number of plug-ins that are ready for you to use on your site.

Plug-ins are what makes WordPress so powerful; plug-ins are small software scripts that can be added to your website and are not included in the initial WordPress installation. WordPress is an open source platform which means anyone can create and develop a plug-in for it to extend its functionality further. There is a wide choice of plug-ins available to install from contact forms, slideshow galleries and even spell-checking. There is a plug-in for any required functionality. It is important to note that having too many plug-ins can slow down your website significantly and can cause conflicts between them. It is best not to have more than 15 plug-ins running at one time.

How to install and manage plug-ins

WordPress has a dedicated section for plug-ins and this can be found in the Dashboard by clicking **Plugins** in the side bar menu:

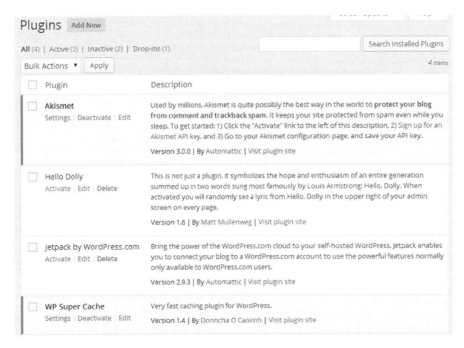

From the plug-ins page you can view, install, activate, or delete plug-ins. When you first install WordPress, it comes with some default plug-ins. These are the

Akismet, Hello Dolly, Jetpack, and WP Super Cache. The Akismet plug-in helps protect your site from spam, and we have already activated this with a unique key. The Hello Dolly plug-in doesn't really do anything and has been included to help you test the plug-in system. You can remove this plug-in by clicking on Delete just under the plug-in title. WordPress will ask you to confirm that you want to delete the plug-in - confirm by clicking **Yes, Delete these files** and the plug-in will be removed from your site. Notice that the activated plug-ins do not have a delete option, that's because you cannot delete active plug-ins, you have to first deactivate the plug-in and then the delete option will appear. To install a plug-in just click on the **Add New** button at the top of the page and you will be taken to the Install Plug-ins page:

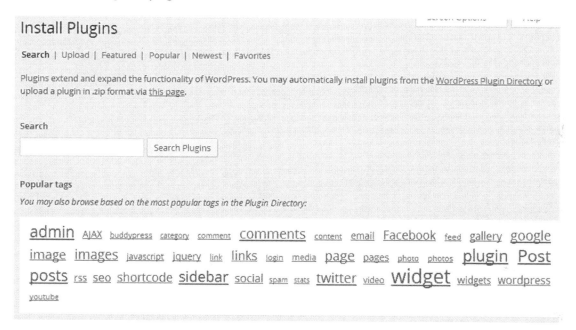

The install plug-ins page lets you install plug-ins in several ways; the first option is to search for the plug-in by name or you can install a plug-in that you have already downloaded by selecting upload. You can also install a featured, popular or the newest plug-in directly from the plug-in directory in WordPress.org. Let's install our first plug-in, in the search box type in "Yoast". This is an SEO plug-in that will help optimize your content for search engines. On the search results page it should be the first one title: 'WordPress SEO by Yoast':

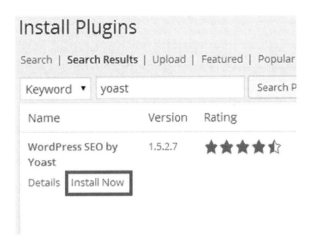

To install the plug-in, just click on Install Now, and WordPress will install the plug-in just like installing a theme. You can activate from this page, just click on Activate Plug-in:

Once the plug-in has been activated, you will be redirected to the plug-ins page and the Yoast SEO plug-in will display a message asking whether you want to allow tracking of the plug-in remotely to help with improvements and support. You don't have to allow tracking but since it is for support and troubleshooting purposes, you should allow tracking:

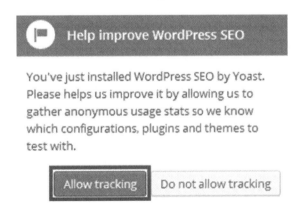

The plug-ins page lets you see which plug-ins you have installed and you can see what plug-ins are active and inactive, with a number next to each at the top of the page:

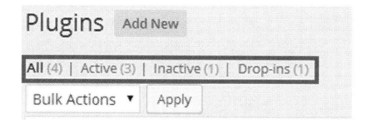

You can also perform actions on multiple plug-ins by using the Bulk Actions dropdown option. To use this, you will have to select the plug-ins from your installed plug-ins by checking the box next to the plug-in title. You can then choose to activate, deactivate, update or delete the selected plug-ins.

How to find good plug-ins

Finding good WordPress plug-ins can be time consuming, because there are so many plug-ins available to choose from. You can get more in-depth details about plug-in by going to the details page of that plug-in. In our previous example, we installed the Yoast SEO plug-in. In the result page before you install, you can click on Details to go to the details page of the plug-in:

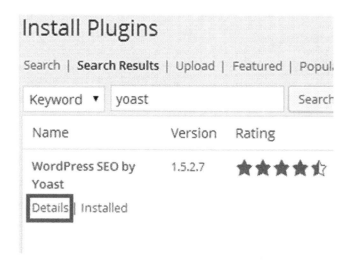

You will then be taken to the details page of that plugin:

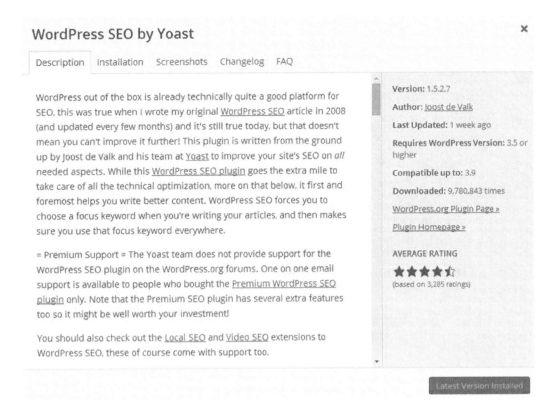

When you are looking for a plug-in, you need to make sure that you carefully consider some important details about the plug-in. For all plug-ins, you should make sure to consider the following metrics:

1. **Check** the **WordPress version.** The first thing you should be looking out for is the version of WordPress that the plug-in requires. On the details page of the plug-in, it will specify the minimum version of WordPress that your site needs to use the plug-in.

2. **Check Compatibility.** Hundreds of plug-ins have been abandoned by their developers and are still floating around the WordPress plug-in directory. To avoid installing these potentially hazardous plug-ins, you need to check the latest supported WordPress version that the plug-in supports. In the details page of the plug-in, you can find this information next to the "compatible up to".

3. **Last Updated.** This is a very important metric to consider, because it shows you when the plug-in was last updated. In our SEO Yoast plug-in, it says that it was updated last week. When a plug-in is regularly updated, this means that there is on-going support and the plug-in is updated to be compatible with the latest version of WordPress and any bugs or security holes have been fixed.

The details page also offers tabs that explain the installation process and the FAQs about the plug-in.

Enhancing your website using core plug-ins

There are thousands of plug-ins available. It can be overwhelming when you install WordPress for the first time and I would like to provide you with some recommendations for some general plug-ins that are essential to any site.

SEO Plug-in

Search Engine Optimization is a very important part of a website's life and you need to have a plug-in that will help optimize your site for the search engines by creating and submitting a sitemap automatically. The sitemap simply lists all of the pages and posts on your site. A useful plug-in is the Yoast WordPress plug-in and you can get the plug-in here: www.wordpress.org/plugins/wordpress-seo.

Anti-Spam Plug-in

Getting traffic is always important and is a good thing for your website, but it also brings the attention of spam bots which will spam your comments. You need to have some kind of protection from this and GASP plug-in is fast becoming one of the great plug-ins for anti-spam. You can get the plug-in here: www.wordpress.org/plugins/growmap-anti-spambot-plugin.

Backup Plug-in

As with anything technology-related, it is very important that you back up your data files on your website. WordPress uses a database to store the pages, posts and comments. BackupBuddy is an important plug-in that will back up your WordPress website on a regular basis, so should your website be taken down or hacked then you can be back up and running quickly. You can get the plug-in here: www.ithemes.com/purchase/backupbuddy.

Contact Plug-in

Every website needs a contact form for users to contact the site owner or to submit information; a useful plug-in is the Contact Form 7- a simple and customizable contact plug-in that can be used on any WordPress website. You can get the plug-in here: www.wordpress.org/plugins/contact-form-7.

Captcha Plug-in

Another tool in the arsenal of web masters in preventing unwanted spam is Captcha - whenever there is data to be submitted anywhere on your website then it is vulnerable to spam bots. You want to make sure that only humans are able to send the data on the form and to do this you can use a simple Captcha plug-in that will add a random key to the Contact 7 plug-in. You can get the plug-in here: www.wordpress.org/plugins/really-simple-captcha.

Sharebar Plug-in

Social networks have taken off in recent times and there is an abundance to choose from. Thousands of users are signed up to these networks and have many contacts that they share things with. To utilize the social networks to get traffic to your website, you need a plug-in that will enable your visitors to share your content with their friends on the social networks such as Facebook, Twitter and Google +. Sharebar is a cool social plug-in that floats vertically on the side of your website and displays the most popular social media buttons to remind people to share your content. You can get the plug-in here: www.wordpress.org/plugins/sharebar.

Group related posts Plug-in

When the content on your website develops, it is good practice and easier for your users to find content by grouping related posts. The WordPress related posts plug-in will create a list of related posts below every post. It also lets you choose how many you want to display. This will encourage your visitors to read more of your content. You can get the plug-in here: http://goo.gl/m2Tioz

Speed up the load process Plug-in

When you have a large volume of content on your website like text, images and video it can take your pages some time to load and your visitors might get frustrated and go to another website. There is a useful plug-in that you can use to speed up the loading time that will load up static pages instead of PHP. You can get the plug-in from here: www.wordpress.org/plugins/wp-super-cache.

Re-use old content Plug-in

When you want to re-use your old content but don't want to manually post them, you can use Tweet Old Post plug-in to automatically tweet your old posts randomly to Twitter. You can get the plug-in here: http://goo.gl/ZPli6u

Premium plug-ins

You are not limited to the WordPress plug-ins directory for your plug-in needs. There are a number of companies that sell plug-ins. You might find that the plug-ins available in the WordPress directory don't meet the requirement that you want, or they are too generic. This is when you will need to use premium plug-ins. You can find premium plug-ins either by searching online, or using recommended companies. You can find premium plug-ins at wppluginplug-ins.com or codecanyon.net.

Chapter 7: Bring Your Content to Life

The Media Library

WordPress isn't just about a bunch of plain posts - you can bring your content to life by utilizing the powerful WordPress media library. The expectations of typical website today are that it must include rich media, such as images, slideshows, videos, and webcasts. WordPress makes it very easy to add rich media content to your website without resorting to writing any code. WordPress gives you many tools to add rich media to your posts and pages with just simple drag & drop and shortcuts. The media library holds all your media content such as pictures, audio and video. You can upload all the media content that you will use on your site into the media library and then WordPress will make this content available to your posts and pages. To get to the media library, just click on **Media** from the Dashboard and you will be taken to your site's media library:

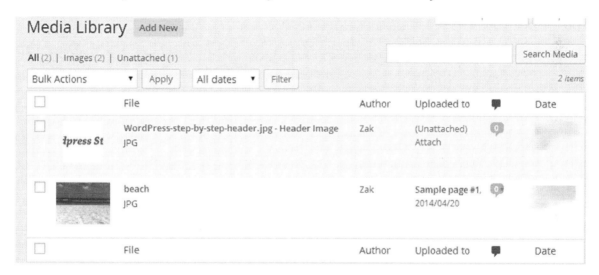

In our media library, we don't have much media content - only the header image and the image used in our sample post. Four columns display the details about the content available in the library. The first column is the File column and this shows us the file name of the media. Next is the Author column and this field displays the author or the person who uploaded the content. The final two columns are the Uploaded to and the Date. The Uploaded to column tells us if the media content is attached to a page or post somewhere on our website, and it provides a link to the location showing what it is attached to. On our site, we have one image that is attached to one post and one image is not attached to anything. This is the header image. The final column shows the date the image was uploaded.

How to upload media

Uploading media onto the media library involves just dragging and dropping a file onto the WordPress, media upload page. You can also upload files by browsing from your computer to add a new media item to the library just click the **Add New** button at the top of the page and WordPress will take you to the Upload New Media page:

WordPress gives you two options to upload media files - you can either drag and drop a file from your computer into the rectangle area or you can select the files by clicking on **Select Files** button and browsing for the image on your computer. Whichever method you use, the media will be uploaded by WordPress into the media library and it will give you an option to edit any pictures that you have just uploaded. Click the **Edit** link next to the media file. I have uploaded a picture of the WordPress logo and WordPress takes me to the Edit media page for the image I just uploaded:

The edit media page gives you several options to edit the media item that you have uploaded. In the above screen shot, I have the WordPress logo that I just uploaded.

1. Right at the top is the title of the image. You can change the name of the image easily from this box.

2. This is the Save box, and it also shows details about the file such as when it was uploaded, file type, file size and file dimensions. You can save the changes you make to the image by clicking the **Update** button.

3. You can click this button to edit the images dimensions. When you click this button, it will open an additional box inside the Edit page and you can specify the images size, crop, and the thumbnail settings:

4. In the caption box, you can write a brief description of the image. This will be displayed when you mouse over the image.

5. The alternative text is used when someone has switched off images on their browser. This is very useful for text readers that help the visually impaired to access content on websites.

6. You can enter detailed descriptions of the media file here.

WordPress creates a unique URL for all of the media content that you uploaded. This makes it very easy to share your rich media content - just click the button under the title box **Get Shortlink** and you can copy the files direct URL:

You can then paste this onto your browser and WordPress will direct you to the image. Once you have finished editing the file, just click the update button and all your changes will be saved. To go back to the media library page, just click on **Media** from the side bar. The user interface in WordPress is consistent across many of the different features. Just as you can apply changes to multiple posts by using the Bulk Actions dropdown menu, you can do the same with the media files. You can go into the edit page of any file that you have in the media library by clicking its title.

How to create great looking posts

Posts are essential to all WordPress websites; they are the meat of your content and you need to make sure that your posts look the best they can and provide your reader with appealing and engaging content. To make posts stand out on your site, you need to utilize formatting, incorporate rich media and utilize the host of features that WordPress provides. When you have lots of content on your site, you can show previews of the posts on your homepage without showing the whole post.

The formatting toolbar

WordPress offers a simple toolbar that is like the toolbar available in a word processor. The toolbar lets you format text exactly the same way you would format it in a word processor. Just like you would format text in word processor, you highlight the word or sentence that you wish to format and add formatting such as bold, underline or italicize. The tool bar offers so many features to format text. Let's have a detailed look at the features available in the toolbar. First, make sure to display all the icons available; you can do this by clicking the toolbar toggle icon:

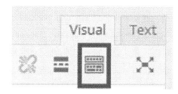

This will display a second line with more toolbar icons. The toolbar provides all the formatting features that you need to create great looking posts. Let's have a brief look at the different toolbar icons available and what they do.

Add media

You can bring your posts to life by adding media content in the form of pictures, audio and video. The add media button lets you do this, you can retrieve media already uploaded onto your media library or you can upload content and put it on your post.

Bold, italic, strikethrough and lists

Just as you would see in a word processor, you have the options to format your text in exactly the same way as you have become accustomed to.

Block quote, horizontal line and alignment

You can recreate the intricate layout that was once only achieved using HTML markup code.

Insert links, create snippets and writing mode

You can create links to external resources just by highlighting text and clicking on the Insert link icon. You can also create a snippet by using the Read more tag next to the Remove link icon. This enables you to show a preview of a post with a link to read more. I will show you how to use this icon later on. The last icon offers you the ability to write in distraction free mode. When you click this icon, WordPress will go to full screen mode and you will be able to concentrate just on your post:

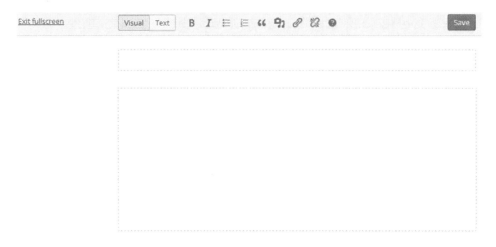

Paragraph

Readers are used to reading organized and well-presented text from offline sources such as newspapers and magazines; therefore, it is important that you present your content by following the formatting rules that readers have become accustomed to. When you're writing a long blog post, you need to make sure that you subdivide the writing into smaller sections, and separate these sections by using subheadings. WordPress offers the Paragraph icon to create subheadings with different sizes. The Paragraph Dropdown Menu gives you six levels of heading to choose from, with heading 1 being the largest heading and decreasing in size as you go up heading levels until heading 6.

Text color, justify, paste, and clear formatting

You can add color to text by using the text color icon and you can choose from 40 colors. The Justify option has also been included, which means that you can make your posts justified. WordPress now has the Paste option as plain text mode, and this means that when you copy and paste from a word processor, your content will be pasted as plain text until you toggle this option off. You can turn this off by clicking the Toggle icon again.

Special characters

The Special Character icon in the toolbar lets you insert special characters that you don't usually see on a standard keyboard. When you click this icon, WordPress will open a new window that displays all of the available characters - just mouse over a character and you can see an enlarged preview on the right:

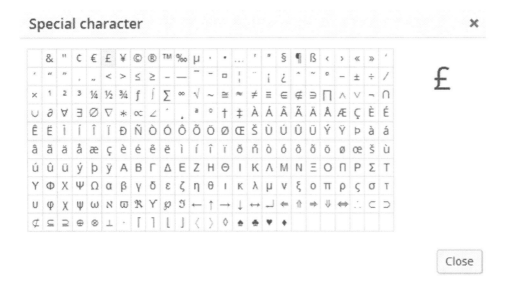

You can easily insert the character you wish to use just by clicking it and WordPress will insert the special character where you left the cursor in the post body.

Indent, undo/redo, and help

The final five icons in the toolbar let you add or remove indent space for a paragraph with the Indent icons. The Undo and Redo icons are useful in undoing or redoing a change. The last icon with the question mark lets you get some help and a list of useful keyboard shortcuts.

HTML and Visual view

You can switch between visual view which gives you a WYSIWG editor and HTML view by clicking on the tabs at the top of the toolbar. When you click on Text, the toolbar will change to display HTML shortcuts that you can click and WordPress will insert the markup automatically in the text area:

Post format

WordPress gives you further options in styling your posts with post formats. This feature styles different types of posts in different ways. Most themes support post formats, and the theme that we are using - the Twenty Twelve - has some basic post format options. The option to choose a post format is on the right with a box title Format. In the Twenty Twelve theme that we are using, you can choose from six different post formats; standard, Aside, Image, Link, Quote, and Status:

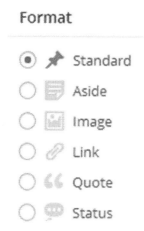

Standard

This is the default post format in WordPress and can apply to an article, blog post, or any other type of content. You can still incorporate any of the other post formats as well, so you can add images, links and quotes. The only difference would be that you can designate a post format by making it an image format, to show the focus of this post is images.

Aside
This post format is used to provide extra information, which is useful since you don't want to write a whole post if your intention is to provide extra bits of information. This could be an external link, reference to a discussion carried out elsewhere on the web, or any other kind of content.

Image
This post format is used to display an image; it is different from a gallery format where you can add multiple images in a WordPress post.

Link
As the name suggests this post format contains a link to a web location. You would typically use this when you want to share a link instead of writing a full post. When you use the link format, you add the title of the link and the URL and a short description of the link.

Quote
The quote post format, as you guessed, is used for quotations. You can use the block quote icon from the toolbar to highlight the quote.

Status
Social networks have become ubiquitous, and even WordPress now supports a status post format which is like a twitter feed status update. But, with the status post format, you are not limited to 140 characters - you write a longer status update.

How to add pictures to posts

The saying "a picture speaks a thousand words" couldn't be more applicable when it comes to creating engaging posts that readers will love. WordPress gives you several different ways to display pictures, and it is rare to see a WordPress website that does not use pictures to enhance the content on the site. To add pictures to a post, first click in the **Edit box** and position the cursor where you want to add the picture. Then click on the **Add Media** button just under the post title and you will be taken to the media library. From here, you can either choose a picture you have already uploaded, insert an image from a URL, or upload a picture from your computer. I have some images already uploaded so I will select a picture from the Media library:

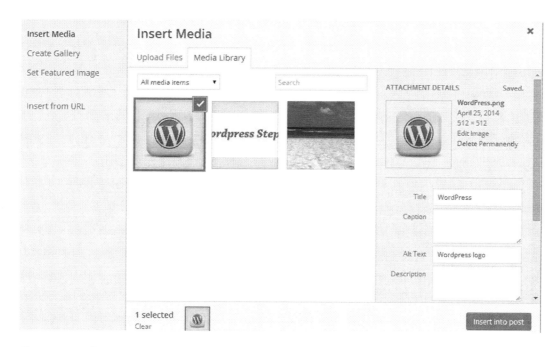

Once you have selected an image, you can insert it as-is into the post by clicking **Insert into post** button or you can edit the image by clicking on the **Edit image** link on the right. Once you have inserted the image, WordPress gives you further options to resize the image visually inside the post. You can also change the alignment by selecting the image and aligning it left, center or right:

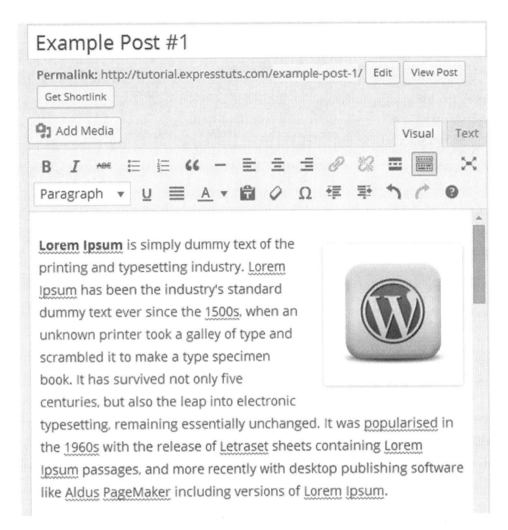

If you still want to further edit the image you can do so, by clicking the image and WordPress will display two options to delete or go into the edit page of the image:

In edit page of the image, WordPress gives you options to add caption, alternative text and to specify image alignment. If you are confident with your CSS coding skills, then WordPress also gives you an advanced settings option where you can add custom CSS styling to a style sheet:

Featured image

Featured images are a popular feature on all WordPress websites, also known as thumbnails they are supported by virtually all themes and some have special built in support for them. The theme that we are using supports featured images, and you can easily find out if a theme supports this feature, inside the add new post or edit page look for a box that says featured image:

Adding a featured image is simple. Just click on the **Set Featured Image** link inside the edit post page, and you will then be taken to the Set Featured Image page. This is the media library and you can select or upload an image that you want to use as the featured image for the post. Once you have chosen which image you want to use as the featured image, just click on **Set Featured Image** button and the image that you chose should now appear under the Featured Image box:

WordPress will resize the image accordingly, but this could mean that the image you choose might appear a little different because different themes handle featured images with their own settings. You should utilize this excellent feature for your posts, as the image will appear next to the post and this enriches your content visually.

How to divide a post into multiple pages

When creating your first post, you learned that you can use the more tag to show a snippet of the post and add a Read More link to access the rest of the post. You can use another technique within WordPress that lets you divide a long post into multiple sections, within the same post. To do this, you can use the nextpage tag: <!--nextpage-->. To use this tag, you need to switch to the HTML view and then insert the tag where you want to start the new page. When you switch back to the visual editor, the nextpage tag will show up as a gray line with the words "Page break" above it. Let's put this to action on our post:

generate Lorem Ipsum which looks reasonable. The generated Lorem Ipsum is therefore always free from repetition, injected humour, or non-characteristic words etc.

Lorem Ipsum is simply dummy text of the printing and typesetting industry. Lorem Ipsum has been the industry's standard dummy text

The page break tells you where the new page will start from, and if we look at the frontend of our site you will see that WordPress conveniently arranges the pages into multiple sections and enables you to switch between these sections via numbered tabs at the bottom of the page:

combined with a handful
looks reasonable. The ger
injected humour, or non-

Pages: 1 2

This is a nice feature, as it lets you divide a long post into multiple sections without having to write another post.

Static v Dynamic sites

In the old days of the web, you would find thousands of static websites on many different topics, but this has changed and the web now has a plethora of websites that are dynamic. When creating your WordPress site, it is important that you understand the difference between static and dynamic sites. Static websites are created once and they do not change. Static sites are usually created manually with HTML and CSS. With static sites, you have to manually add content, so if you wanted to add a new article you would do so using HTML markup and CSS to style it, although you can have a style sheet for your whole website. On the other hand, dynamic websites generate content on the fly, this means that your content is stored in a database and then a scripting language, such PHP, is used to dynamically generate the content by date, category, keyword tag, etc. A WordPress website is an example of a dynamic website that uses a database and scripting software to generate pages.

Therefore, when you click on the homepage of a WordPress site you are taken to a dynamically generated page that lists all of the posts in reverse chronological order. With dynamic sites, you have no control over the order of the content, as it was dynamically generated by date with the newest content appearing first. WordPress was originally created to cater for news based websites, where the newest content is always displayed at the top, but if you don't want your site to behave like this, WordPress gives you the option to switch to a static site, and you can have more control over the order of the content and how it's laid out. This is what makes WordPress truly flexible; you can use it as both a static and dynamic website.

Home page: static or blog?

Now that you know the difference between static and dynamic sites, you need to decide whether you want to have a static homepage or a blog style homepage. You can choose how you want WordPress to behave from the **Reading** settings under **General settings**, as you've seen before. Personally, I like to have a static homepage, where I can control what goes on the homepage, because not every WordPress site needs to function like a full blown news blog. For example, if you had a website that teaches your visitors something, it might not be suitable for you to use the blog layout style, as all of the content would be arranged in reverse chronological order and this would make it confusing for your readers to find relevant content; important pages would get buried and lost as time went on. This would make your WordPress site very difficult to navigate, and it would make sense to use static pages for some of your content, and make this available through your home page. It is possible to use WordPress as both a blog and static website; you can do this by changing your homepage to a static layout. Refer back to the reading settings to see how you can set your homepage as a static or blog layout.

What are Embeds and Shortcodes?

If you look around, you will see that the top websites are splattered with rich media, including slideshows, video clips, webcasts, audio and podcasts. Before WordPress, adding these features was the domain of computer geeks, as this involved adding chunky code into your web pages. But, with WordPress, adding these features will become second nature in minutes, as WordPress equips you with features to enrich your post with media much quicker than the time it took you to write them. We'll have a look at the few ways that WordPress lets us add rich media to our site.

Embeds and Shortcodes let you add special types of content, such as slideshows and videos into your posts and pages without writing a single line of code - WordPress will do that for you. WordPress now has an excellent new feature that embeds the real media into your post or page just by adding the URL link of that resource. Let's say that you want to embed a YouTube video inside your post. Before, you would have to get the embed code from YouTube and paste this inside your post whilst in HTML view. Now, WordPress will automatically embed the real media just by using the URL of that resource.

How to embed video into a post

To see this in action I'm going to add a YouTube video to a post. Inside the post, I'm just going to paste the link of the YouTube video directly into the post, and then click **Publish** and the **View Post** button next to the permalink to see the results:

How to embed video into a post

The result is a beautiful post with the YouTube video embedded just by using the URL of the video. You can do the same thing with pictures - just paste the URL of the image, and WordPress will automatically embed the picture into your post or page. Adding videos and pictures using automatic embed is easy enough, but there are some basic criteria that you need to be aware of for embeds to work.

1. Put the URL on a separate line. WordPress needs to be able to identify that this is a URL link and that it should be embedded automatically. It can only do this if the URL is on a line of its own. Make sure that you do not put text next to the URL, as that will cause the automatic embed not to work.

2. Don't format the URL as a link. WordPress needs to be able to differentiate the links pointing to a resource on the web or on your site from the links that you want to use as embeds. Formatting a link involves using a special HTML tag and when you do this, WordPress will not display an Embed, but a link instead.

3. The site you are embedding from must be on the WordPress list. The auto-embed feature only works for a number of sites that WordPress has included; this is a security measure to protect your WordPress sites from hackers. The list is ever increasing and WordPress will continue to add more sites, but rest assured the most popular sites are all covered. These include: YouTube, Flickr, Hulu, Instagram Vimeo, and Twitter. You can check to see the full list here: http://codex.wordpress.org/Embeds.

Shortcodes

Shortcodes work in a slightly different way but give you broader options and let you add specialized content to your WordPress site. Shortcodes are the special tags that you can enter directly into a post, and WordPress will generate specialized content when the post is viewed in the frontend. WordPress will use a shortcode when you add a gallery to your post and it replaces the shortcode with the code needed to display a gallery of images. Shortcodes are similar to HTML tags; they are enclosed with square brackets, e.g. [gallery]. With a little bit of tweaking and adding code to one of your WordPress files, you can create your own custom Shortcodes that display pretty much anything.

How to create a gallery

As we previously mentioned, you can use a built in shortcode to create a gallery within your post. To do this click on **Add Media** button and select **Create Gallery** from the left. You can create a gallery using the pictures that you have uploaded to the media library or you can upload files by clicking the **Upload Files** tab, and either using the drag and drop feature or browse for the image files from your computer:

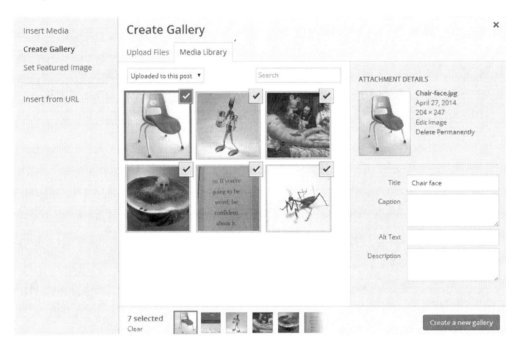

For each image, you can add a title, caption, Alt text and a description. Once you have chosen the pictures that you wish to use, just click on the **Create a new gallery** button and you will be taken to the settings page for your new gallery:

From this page you can choose where you want the image to link to when the user clicks the picture in the gallery, by default WordPress launches an attachment page that displays the larger-size image along with its description, if this was included. You can also specify how many columns you want your gallery pictures to use under the **Columns** options. The final option lets you make the order in which the pictures appear in your post random, so every time you refresh the page the order of the pictures will be random. Let's see how our gallery looks like on the frontend:

Art collection

Once you click an image in the gallery, WordPress will display the attachment page for that picture, and you will see a larger size of the image along with its title, caption and description, if you added one:

Chair face

Published   27, 2014 at 204 × 247 in Art collection. Edit

Next →

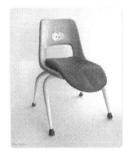

Funny Chair face

This is chair face. Creating this is simple, all you need are a chair with a whole in the back, drawing of eyes and a red cushion pillow.

Thursday

Chapter 8: Open Up Your Site & Enable Users to Log In & Contribute

Over the past ten years, the web has transformed. Gone are the days when you had static, flash and mediocre websites dominating the online space; the web has now become a medium close to how we function in real life. The social networking phenomenon has really taken off in the past decade and on the back of that the need to have a website that enables users to connect with the webmaster. The site's content has really become an essential part of a modern website. WordPress was born amidst this shift on the web, and it makes it possible for you to have friends, colleagues, family members, and even complete strangers to contribute to your site. Much like how a traditional off-line magazine would operate, you can create a site where several people can post content, and WordPress gives you fine control on who writes, reviews and publishes content on your site.

Every WordPress website starts with only a single user, which is the administrator who has access to do pretty much anything on the site. But, as your site grows, and the content that you create needs to be expanded, you may decide that you need to have other people to help you to run your site. These users will be your co-authors, and will be responsible for writing part of your website's content. WordPress gives you five different levels of users on your site. These are:

Administrator. This the super-user who can do anything on a WordPress site without any restrictions. WordPress gives you the option to create multiple administrators that have exactly the same powers as you. This means that they can create posts, change the settings, install a new theme, and they can even remove the original administrator from the site. In terms of best practices, and for security reasons, it is highly recommended that you do not create multiple administrators on your site, and the general rule of thumb is that every WordPress site should only ever have one administrator.

Editor. The next role down the power hierarchy is the editor. An editor on a site can create, edit, and delete posts on the site. Editors also have the power to manage categories, tags, upload files, and moderate and approve comments. The only restriction that editors have is that they can't change site settings, change the site's theme or manage users.

Author. If you have a ghostwriter (someone that writes content on your behalf) then the role that you assign that person on your site will be an author. An author's powers within a WordPress site are only limited to their own posts. This means that they can only create, edit, and delete their own posts.

Contributor. Contributors have even less power than the authors on a WordPress site, essentially they are like authors, but they can only create draft posts, and are not able to publish them. Contributors have to submit their work to the administrator and editor of the site before it is published. Once the administrator and the editor approve the content, they will have the option to publish it so and make it appear on the frontend.

Subscriber. The lowest level is the subscriber. Subscribers can register on the site, and they can opt in to be notified when new content is posted to the site. Subscribers are much like the normal visitors; they cannot do anything on your site, except reading and commenting on posts. The main use for subscribers is if you have membership website, you can restrict access to your content only to registered subscribers.

How to add users to your site

WordPress lets you create users easily from the Dashboard. To create a new user, you need to provide three things:

1. Username

2. Password

3. Email address

In the Dashboard mouse over the **Users** menu on the side bar and then select **Add new**:

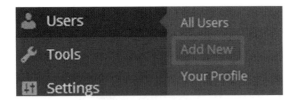

You will be taken to the Add New User page, though WordPress only requires three fields, you will also want to enter the first and last name of the person you are adding to your site:

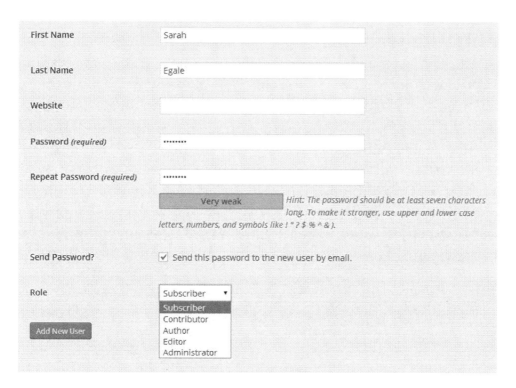

Once you have entered the details, you can decide if you want to send the password to the new user via their email by ticking the checkbox next to **Send this password to the new user by email,** and can select which role you want to assign the new user to from the dropdown menu next to **Role**. When you are finished adding the required details, just click the **Add new user** button, and WordPress will create the new user and take you to the Users page:

We now have an additional user on the site with the role of contributor. From the Users page, you can manage all the users on your site. So, if you want to delete a user that you no longer need, just like deleting a post, you hover your mouse over the username and two options will appear, edit and delete:

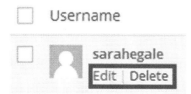

You can also edit the users details by selecting edit, in the edit screen you can update a user's password, set author name, add biographical information and even change the user's role within your site.

Collaborate with authors

Once you have created a user and assigned a suitable role, WordPress lets you collaborate with that user depending on the role that you have assigned to them. The only user role that is not able to write posts are the subscribers. WordPress gives a different admin backend to different users on the site, in terms of publishing posts; this is the same for administrator, editor, and author. The contributor can only write posts, but not publish them. The login process for all user types in WordPress is the same as the administrator, to login www.yoursite.com/wp-admin - where you replace "yoursite" with the URL of your site. The following screen is what a contributor would see when inside the WordPress admin Dashboard:

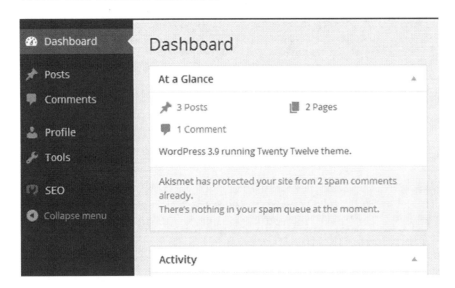

The contributor sees a stripped down version of the dashboard, notice that the contributor only has access to creating posts, but not publishing them, profile, and browsing comments, but not moderating them. There are no options to make changes to the site's theme, widgets, or general settings. All user types can login to the dashboard, but the most stripped down version is the subscriber, as they only have access to the profile page where they can set preferences and personal information.

When a contributor creates a post, they only have a **Submit for Review** button:

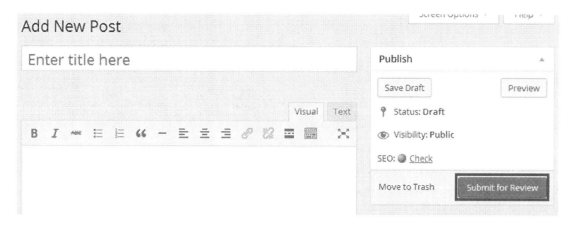

Once the contributor clicks on the **Submit for Review** button, the post is then added to the pending list, and only an administrator or editor can approve the post. An administrator or an editor can then moderate the post. This is very important, as you don't want potentially harmful content to be published on your site. With this method, an administrator or an editor can view the content and even make changes before publishing. To approve a comment an administrator or editor will need to be logged into the Dashboard and then go to the All posts section by hovering the mouse over **Posts** in the side bar menu and selecting **All posts.** From the All posts screen, the administrator or editor can view the post submitted by the contributor by clicking the **Pending** link just under the title:

The pending link will have a number next to it inside brackets; this indicates the number of posts that are awaiting approval. When you go inside the post submitted by the contributor, you can edit it just like you would edit your own posts, and if you are happy with the content you can just click the **Publish** button. This is an excellent feature on WordPress - you can hire someone to write content for your site; add them as a user; view the content they have submitted and when you are happy, publish the content to your site. WordPress really makes collaborating with authors simple.

Get readers to share your content

As we've already mentioned, although content is the lifeblood of your website, this is only half of your job; you now need to get readers to find that great content you've created. Promoting your site has now become just as important as the content itself because it's no good having great content without readers to consume it. In the beginning, promoting yourself and your content will be difficult, but you will find that when you add it to your normal routine when creating content, it will become second nature to you. Promoting yourself involves several factors but the two most important ones are Search Engine Optimization, known as SEO, and getting your users to share your content. I will discuss the former in detail later in the book. But, as for the second aspect, getting your users to share your content is just as important.

When readers share your content with others, this can be the best form of word-of mouth for you and your site, since they clearly like your content, and have taken the time to share it with others. It means that they have personally endorsed you, and this is very powerful. On the web today, sharing involves using the social networking platforms Facebook, Google Plus, Twitter, and YouTube. These social networking platforms are used by millions of people online and when users share your content, it can create exponential exposure and help elevate your authority status online.

It is more than likely that you have come across a great post, and you have noticed the option to share the post with Facebook, Google Plus, Twitter and YouTube to name a few:

With plug-ins, you can encourage users to share your content on your site. The plug-ins that you add to WordPress makes it super easy for your readers to share your content with the use of simple share buttons next to your posts and pages.

How to add Share buttons to your content

To add share button, we need to activate the Jetpack plug-in. This is a great plug-in that now comes pre-installed with WordPress. The Jetpack plug-in brings the features that WordPress.com users use to your self-hosted version of WordPress. Some of the features included in this plug-in include:

- Share buttons for your content for all major social networking platforms
- A widget for displaying recent tweets
- Spell checker
- Monitor your site's activity with notifications

The Jetpack offers many more features, and to see a list of all the features go to: https://wordpress.org/plugins/jetpack/. We're going to use the share buttons that are provided by the Jetpack plug-in. Once you have activated the Jetpack plug-in, you need to connect your site to WordPress.com by clicking the large green button at the top:

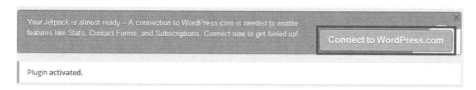

Once you click on the button, you will be taken to the Jetpack authorization page on WordPress.com. Here you need to enter a WordPress.com username and password. If you don't have an account, just create one by clicking the **Need an account?** Link on the right. Signing up for an account is quick and easy, and you can even just sign up for just a username. Once you have entered your credentials, just click **Authorize**. Once authorization is complete, WordPress will redirect you back to the settings page of Jetpack. Your site now has access to a host of features:

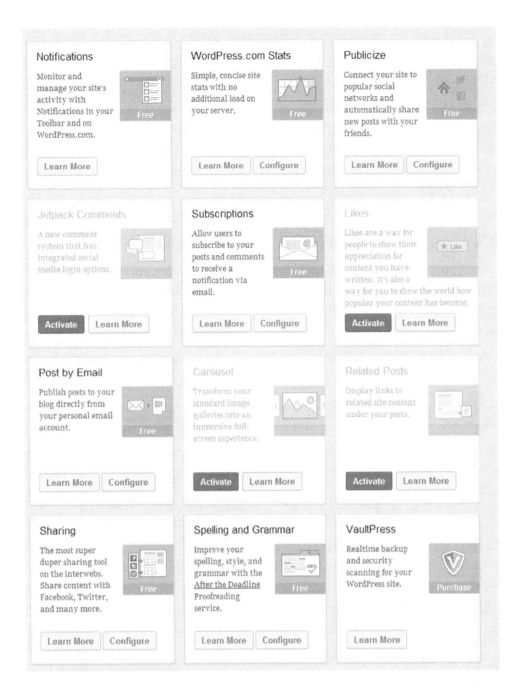

Wordpress also create a dedicated menu for Jetpack in the sidebar menu:

In the submenu (highlighted in red), WordPress lists the options for settings; by default, the three options available are Omnisearch, Site Stats, and Akismet.

There are two ways to get to the share settings inside the Jetpack, you can either scroll down and click on **Configure** under the sharing box:

Or, you can go to **Settings** and then select **Sharing**. Either way, you will be taken to the **Sharing Settings** page. On this page, you can choose which sharing buttons you want to add on your site. So, if you want to add the share buttons for Facebook, Google Plus, and Twitter to your site, you simply drag and drop the button from the Available Services, area into the Enabled Services area:

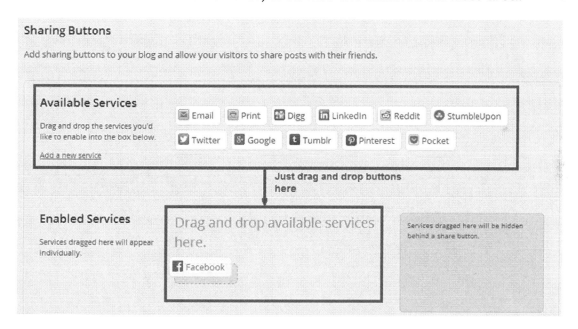

You can select which sharing buttons that you want to add to your site; in most cases, this would include Facebook, Twitter, and Digg/StumbleUpon. It's up to you to which buttons you want to add. WordPress makes this process easy. If there is a service that is missing from the available share buttons, WordPress gives you the option to add the service, and you can do this by clicking the **Add new service link.**

You can also add a print button, to enable your readers to print the content of the post or page directly. Within the Sharing Settings page, WordPress gives you a preview section to show you how your buttons will look on the frontend:

Live Preview

You can arrange the ordering of the button exactly to your preference - just click on the button and drag it where you want. You can add as many or as few share buttons as you wish; if you want to use all of the share buttons available but don't want to cram all of them next to your post, then you can utilize the hidden share button feature that WordPress provides. You can add more share buttons inside the grey area:

Buttons that you put inside here will be hidden behind a "more" button that will reveal all of the buttons inside; this gives you more options to share your content using different social network platforms.

In the settings page, you have more options to customize the share buttons on your site:

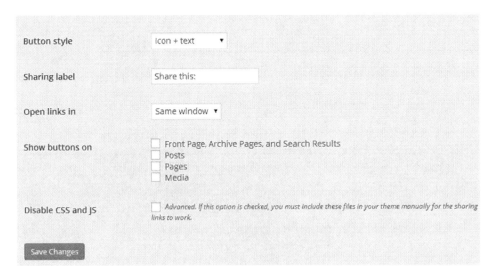

You can choose the button style which gives you four options:

- Icon and text
- Icon only
- Text only
- Official buttons

You can choose the button style by selecting the dropdown menu next to **Button Style**. In the Sharing label dropdown menu, you can select the text that you want to appear next to your sharing buttons. By default, it says "Share this:" but you can customize the label to whatever you like. You can also choose how links are opened - in the same window or a new window. To display the sharing options, choose this from the dropdown menu next to the options **Open Links In**. Next, you have to choose where you want to the share buttons to appear on your site. There are four options to choose from - front page along with archive pages and search results; posts, pages, and media. You can select to have the share buttons appear on all areas or you can select only posts or pages. Finally, there is an option to disable CSS and JavaScript which you should leave unchecked, as you need this enabled for the sharing buttons to work. The next step is to link your social profiles with your sharing buttons. Depending on the social network sharing button you have chosen, just click the **Connect** button next to the network and you will be taken to a new page where you need to log in and allow WordPress to access your social network profile. When prompted, just enter the credentials for the social network in question and click on **Authorize**.

To see how the share buttons will appear in the frontend, just click the **Save Changes** button and visit the frontend of your site:

There are many variations of passages of Lorem Ipsum available, but the majority have suffered alteration in some form, by injected humour, or randomised words which don't look even slightly believable. If you are going to use a passage of Lorem Ipsum, you need to be sure there isn't anything embarrassing hidden in the middle of text. All the Lorem Ipsum generators on the Internet tend to repeat predefined chunks as necessary, making this the first true generator on the Internet. It uses a dictionary of over 200 Latin words, combined with a handful of model sentence structures, to generate Lorem Ipsum which looks reasonable. The generated Lorem Ipsum is therefore always free from repetition, injected humour, or non-characteristic words etc.

Pages: 1 2

The buttons appear at the bottom of the article, and they will appear in the order that you have dictated. Notice the more button; once clicked, this will reveal more sharing buttons and will give the reader more platform options to share your content. The Sharing feature inside the Jetpack plug-in gives you a powerful feature that you can use to create share buttons on your site with just a few clicks.

Chapter 9: Keep Things Running By Securing Your Site

As with any technology available today, there are likely to be security loop holes that will create risks for your WordPress installation. The following are some tips to help you secure your WordPress website.

Back up WordPress

If you ask most people, they will tell you that they have lost valuable data because they didn't create a backup. Losing valuable information is painful and in some cases, this can be a major problem when you lose data worth thousands. As with everything in life, nothing is 100% secure and there will always be hackers around discovering new vulnerabilities in websites. With that said, you can reduce the risk of losing your website by creating a backup. There are many different options to back up your WordPress site and we'll discuss all the options available to you:

1. **Use an automated service.** This is probably the best and most convenient way to back up your WordPress site. Several companies offer automated backups, but the most reliable is Vaultpress - from the same guys that run WordPress.com. Vaultpress will back up and store all of your posts, pages, comments, and settings. You can rollback to any point in the past should disaster strike. This service from Vaultpress will take you back $5 a month for its Lite package; $15 for the basic package and $40 for the premium backup package (figures are correct as of time of this writing). You can check out the packages available here: www.vaultpress.com/plans. Vaultpress is also available through your Jetpack plug-in but like the many other features, you need to activate it and sign up for a monthly plan. Chances are that you are on a tight budget, and coughing up a monthly fee to use Vaultpress might not be an option. Fortunately, the web is full of alternatives and in this case, a nifty plug-in called BackupBuddy. Backupbuddy is a plug-in created by the guys at ithemes.com and you can buy the plug-in for a one-time fee of $80. If you have more than two sites, then you can purchase the freelancer version which lets you back up ten sites. To use Backupbuddy, you need to have access to online storage such as DropBox -dropbox.com, Google drive, and Amazon S3, and the plug-in will back up your site periodically to your chosen online storage medium.

2. **Use a plug-in to manually back up.** The next option is to use a third-party plug-in and make the backups yourself; this is an ideal option if you don't want to fork out money upfront in the beginning. Several excellent plug-ins can help you do this, but most of these plug-ins focus on backing up the database only and you have to back up all of the sites files including the theme files. I highly recommend that you use a plug-in that backs up both your site's files and the database. One plug-in that can do just that, and won't cost you a penny, is BackWPup. This plug-in is one of the best in the business, you can put your backups into Dropbox,

Google drive, and Amazon S3. You can download BackWPup Plug-in from the official WordPress plug-in directory: www.wordpress.org/plugins/backwpup.

Use strong passwords

This is a given - and you should use strong passwords with combinations of upper and lower case letters with numbers and special characters. You should not use passwords that contain common words or phrases and make sure that you do not use the same password on multiple platforms - such as the same password for your email. If your email password is compromised, so will your WordPress website.

Keep WordPress up to date

WordPress.org releases periodic updates and you will be notified of this in the admin panel in the backend - just follow the upgrade link and it will upgrade your WordPress installation. This way you are secured against new security flaws that have been discovered by developers. It is important to make a backup before you initiate any update process as an update could easily break your site.

Keep plug-ins up to date

Like the WordPress installation, plug-ins need to be updated to keep up with security updates. Developers will make updates to their plug-ins and again you will be notified in the admin part of the plug-in.

Password protect your WP-admin folder

You should password protect your WP admin folder and password protecting your folders is a good way to keep any hackers from destroying your files and data.

Hide your plug-ins

To keep hackers from exploiting vulnerabilities in third party plug-ins, you should hide them altogether and you can do this by uploading a blank index.html file into the wp-content/plug-ins directory.

Install limit login attempts

There is a cool plug-in that you can use to limit the number of login attempts on your WordPress website. The plug-in will also block the IP address that repeatedly tries to log into your WordPress website. You can get the plug-in here: http://goo.gl/fdGhDk

Friday

Chapter 10: Attracting Search Engine Traffic

Creating a website nowadays is the easy part. What's become harder to do is get search engines and the rest of the world to discover your great WordPress website. In the old days, it was possible to slap together a website with some pages, add content and wait a few weeks and it would magically appear in Google. Those days are long gone and nowadays you have to promote your site to both readers and search engines in the right way. This process of getting your site discovered by the search engines is called Search Engine Optimization or SEO for short, and is an extremely important part of a website's lifecycle. First and foremost, it is imperative that your site offers great content because as the web has matured over the last few years, your website must stand out from the crowd by offering great content. Another important rule is to make sure that you always update your site with fresh content; people won't bother to visit your site if it has outdated information and has not been updated for a long time.

The importance of accommodating for search engines

The importance of accommodating for search engines when writing your content can not be emphasized enough, as this is the main tool that people will use to get to your site. Search engines have their own rules, and for them to add your site to their list of millions, your site needs to meet basic criteria. The first thing that search engines try to do is analyze the source code text of your site and try to understand what your site is about. Fortunately, WordPress is optimized for search engines and will do much of the leg work in the background to make sure that your site meets the basic requirements. But, completing some basic tasks can further enhance your site's SEO.

Optimize your articles

When creating content on your site, it is important to follow some basic good practices when writing and formatting your posts and pages. When creating a post or a page, make sure that you use a keyword focused title which is meaningful. This is one of the most important aspects when it comes to SEO, as the title of your post or page is what a potential reader will first see. More important, the search engines will index and associate with a phrase that readers search for. Therefore, it is important to use good, strong, meaningful, descriptive, and specific titles. For example, instead of using a post title of "How to lose weight", you could use a specific and clear title such as "7 steps to lose 2lB in a week". The second title is more focused and the reader is more likely to click through to that title since it offers steps, and gives an idea of how much weight the user can lose. Also, you should try to keep your title short. This means that you shouldn't make the title unnecessarily long, as it will be the first line that will be shown in the site description on the search engine's results page.

Use clear formatting

Search engines expect your WordPress posts and pages to be formatted according to the few simple rules that clearly define the structure of your content. This means that you need to explicitly highlight your headings as H1, and not just plain text style as bold, as search engines won't recognize your headings. Search engines scan document headings that follow a hierarchical structure, so it is important that the main page is formatted with a Heading 1 or H1 style. WordPress can apply Heading 1 through to Heading 6 from the WYSIWYG editor's paragraph drop down menu. Search engines give headings more weight than regular text, and this means that you can emphasize keywords by using them in your page headings.

Write Pillar content

Content is the lifeblood of all websites, because without content you will not get visitors. The best and most successful websites have rich, authentic and quality content that engages users. We will discuss some tips that will help you create great content and encourage your readers to read and share! Pillar content is tutorial-related content that has step by step detailed instructions that are easy to follow and understand. To use shoes as an example of pillar content, we might have: '*10 awesome shoes that you must have*'. To make the post useful you could link to an external link for each shoe type where they can buy the shoes and you can earn a share of the sale as an affiliate. Pillar content and list posts are very popular as they are easy to follow and understand. Popular pillar content is shared among readers via social media. It is also important that pillar content isn't merely listing a bunch of ideas and tips, but actually backing this up with real examples and this will make the post more useful to readers.

Ask your readers

The success of a WordPress website is often measured by how active the readers are - it is therefore a good idea to write posts that facilitate discussion. This works well when you write lists posts, as in our previous example of the 10 must-have shoes - you can end the post by asking the readers to come up with the 11th or a complete alternative to your list with justification. This will engage your readers and people love giving their feedback and their opinions on a subject matter. This shows that you are thoughtful and care about your readers' thoughts and opinions. It is not always advisable to create these kinds of posts when you have a new website, as you will have low traffic and won't generate discussion. However, once you have good traffic, these kinds of posts will form an integral part of your website content.

Be unique and controversial

When you look at successful blogs - they all have one thing in common which is that they are not afraid to be controversial. You need to spice up your website and controversial content which goes against common doctrine will generate attention and comments. If you have a stance on a controversial topic that is related to your niche, then you can write about this in a post either defending or attacking this stance. There is a fine line between alienating your audience and writing about controversial subjects; you need to exercise good judgment and make sure that you are open to their opinions.

Images

Images are an integral part of your online content and people often underestimate the amount of traffic that images can bring. People online search images as well as web pages through search engines, therefore it is important that you use tags, captions and titles to describe your images. There are plenty of SEO plug-ins that automatically update all of your images with proper ALT and TITLE tags for SEO - just search the official WordPress plug-in directory.

Body content

In the main body content of your posts and pages, you need to both ensure that you use keywords appropriately, repeating them sufficiently, and that your content makes sense – it must not just be a repetition of the keywords only. You should mention your targeted phrase in the first paragraph and then throughout the body; you should use variations and words related to the phrase. You have to remember that you are writing for humans, not the search engine robots. You need to strike a healthy balance between writing to be ranked on the search engines and writing for your human audience. When writing or editing your posts or pages, you should ask yourself which words your visitors would use when searching for content that you are writing for. Think of all the possible search terms, synonyms, and abbreviations that different types of visitors might use to find your content. Google's Keyword Planner is an excellent tool to help you identify which keywords you should use in your posts and pages.

Guest posting

This is making a post on another website that already has traffic and a steady readership. This is a popular, free way to attract a new audience to your website. If you find a popular website connected to your niche, whose owner is willing to accept a guest post, then this can be a good way to attract some free traffic for your website. Most websites will allow you to add a short biography about yourself and a link to your website.

Comment on other sites

Commenting is a simple strategy that will help get your website noticed. However, it is very important that it is done properly and this will have a good impact on your website.

Comment on related sites

This is something that goes without saying, but you don't want to comment on sites that are not related to your topic or niche. People tend to focus on quantity rather than quality and comment on any and every website that they come across. When you comment on websites that are related to your niche, you have a very high chance of attracting visits from people who are interested in your content.

Comment early

Commenting on large websites with high traffic is likely to bring many visitors to your website; if you comment early, people will likely see your comment and are likely to visit your website. Most site owners have a publishing schedule, so if you can find out when they post, you can try to ensure that you are one of the first comments on the post.

Use a good opening sentence

As with headlines, make sure that you start your comment with an opening sentence that will grab the attention of the reader.

Disagree

In most cases, comments will agree with the main article, but when you are opposed to the main idea of the post and you can back this up with solid evidence, you are sure to get attention.

Good spelling, grammar and format

Make sure that your comment is well formatted and does not have grammatical errors. Most websites will allow you to insert standard formatting like <strong> and italics. You should highlight key points by making them bold. This is even more important for long comments, as long comments can also draw in more readers to your website.

Comment regularly

Popular sites will have many readers and when you are commenting regularly and become a solid contributor, people will take notice and start to visit your website to read more of your work. It is important that your comments are related to the topic at hand and are not just written for the sake of commenting.

Use social media

Social media plays a crucial role in helping a website to become a success. There are now companies dedicated to the work of social media and helping websites with their social media needs. Regardless of which social media platform that you use - Twitter, Facebook, or Google +, you need to make sure that you keep your followers connected. The best way is to engage people and be helpful, as social media can help make sales indirectly.

Facebook

One of the foremost social media platforms is Facebook which will help you stay connected with your fans. Facebook has Millions and Millions of users and is suited to discussions and interactions. You can create a Facebook page for your website where readers can follow you and you can update them on new events and contests on your website. The following are some tips for using Facebook:

- Post often
- Start Discussions
- Respond to wall posts
- Activate the Facebook fan box widget via your Jetpack plug-in

Twitter

Twitter is a different kind of animal to Facebook and allows you to send messages that are 140 characters or less; it is a microblogging social site. The following tips will help you to utilize Twitter:

- Create a profile with a picture and short bio
- Tweet relevant articles in your niche
- Interact and follow others
- Use Tweriod to see when is the best time to send out your tweets

Twitter is a powerful social media platform and if you utilize its many features, you will increase the visitors to your website.

Google plus

Google + is new to the social networking arena and it is Google's answer to Facebook. The way Google + works is that you put friends or "connections", as Google calls it, into circles that you want to share information with. Google has a nice feature called Hangouts which will let you hold private conversations in text, audio and video with a select group of people. Google, as you know, has the best search engine on the web and if you can integrate your SEO techniques with Google + you can rank higher in search engine results as Google will always favor its own social platform against Facebook or others. Some tips for Google: +

- Create a profile - this is easy to do. Make sure you add as much detail as possible
- Add circles
- Start chatting - try to start conversation with high profile people

YouTube

Many people neglect the power of YouTube - you can get free traffic via YouTube, and the best way to use it is to be helpful and your video will reach thousands of people. The good thing about YouTube is that it allows you to use keywords to describe your video. You can look at popular YouTube videos, create your own one and then tag them with similar keywords in your description of the video. It is important that you create videos that your audience will want to watch. Here are some tips for using YouTube to drive traffic to your website:

- Use descriptive titles, descriptions and keywords for your video - this will help you get found on YouTube and Google
- Embed your videos into related posts and pages on your website
- In the description field, add your website URL - users can click through to your website after watching your video
- Use screen recording software such as Camtasia or Camstudio to create How to tutorials
- Create video responses - look for popular videos in your niche and create a video response

Link your posts internally

Have you come across a post and noticed there are several links within the post that direct you to different, but related posts? This is called internal linking of posts - it will help you to keep your visitors on your site longer. Internal linking is more suitable when your site grows and you have lots of content to display, but has also been known to help with Search Engine Optimization. When you link your pages together, it helps SEO bots to see content on your site through your inter-linking structure. When the SEO bots visit your site, they need to have access to a crawlable link structure that lets them browse the pathways of a website in order to find all of the pages on the website. Therefore, it is important that you inter-link your posts on your website, and allow the SEO bots to add your sites pages to their database. In WordPress, you can add a link to another post on your site by using the link icon in the WYSIWYG toolbar. To link to another related post, simply highlight the text that you wish to use as the link and then click on the link icon from the toolbar:

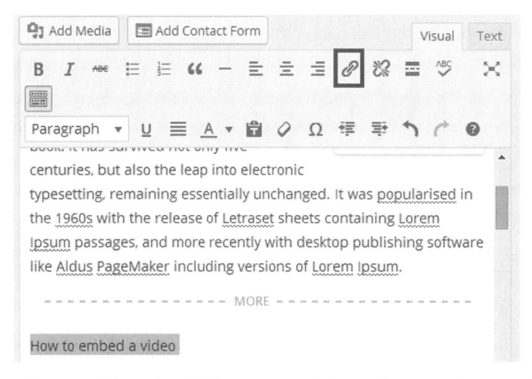

When you click on the link icon, a new window will open and you can link to an external or internal resource. We want to link to another post, so just click on the **Link to existing content** link and WordPress will expand the window to search for the resource you want to link to or choose from the list:

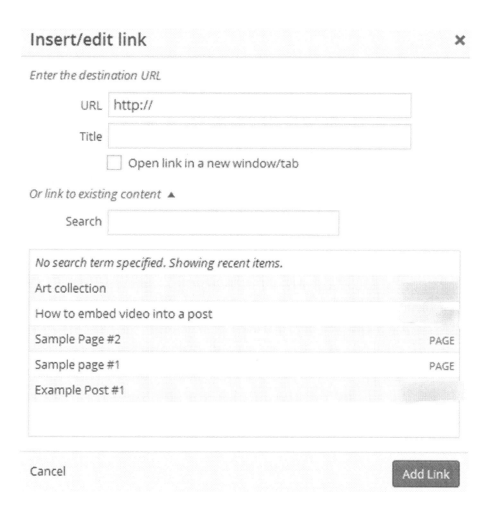

If you use the search feature, WordPress will give you a dropdown list of matching keywords and you can choose a post, or you can just select the post you want to link to from the list. You can specify how WordPress opens the link; external links are better opened in a new window. Once you have highlighted the post that you want to link to, just click on the **Add Link button**. The text that you selected as the link is now blue and underlined to indicate that this is a link, and the reader can now click through to another post on your site:

Letraset sheets containing Lorem I
recently with desktop publishing s
Lorem Ipsum.

How to embed a video

You can also create links to your other posts using a plug-in that will create a link to related posts. One of the best plug-ins in the business for this is the Yet Another Related Posts Plug-in, YARPP for short. YARPP supports can display related posts using thumbnails and textual links. You can get the free plug-in from the official WordPress plug-in directory at YARPP.

Monitoring Site visitors

Quality content and visitors are what keeps a website alive, because without these two things a website will quickly cease to exist. As your site grows, you need to make sure that you keep track of the visitors, where they came from, what keywords they used to get to your site, etc. Keeping track of your site' statistics will also help you to understand which promotion strategies are working and how this is affecting your site. Several WordPress plug-ins and external applications such as Google Analytics can track your site's visitors. However, the easiest option that is already available to you is the site stats feature on the Jetpack plug-in. To get to the Site Stats page, hover the mouse over **Jetpack** on the side bar in the Dashboard and then select **Site Stats**:

You will then be taken to the site stats page. From here, you can see detailed statistics of your site's visitors. Please note that this will be empty initially, as there are no visitors to the site yet. But, once your site is populated, the stats page will update and the page will come alive!

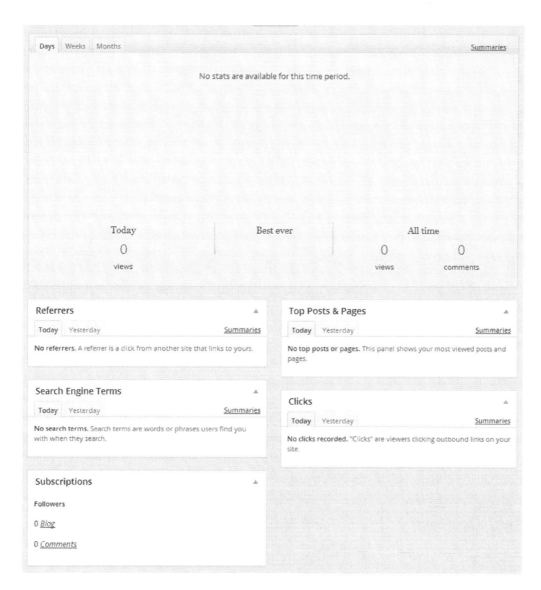

The stats page shows you statistics based on different metrics. You can see detailed stats on:

- Referrers
- Top posts & pages
- Search engine terms
- Clicks

Each of these metrics has a box dedicated to show the stats. The Referrers stats box shows you the number of external referrers that link to your site. Top Posts and Pages box shows the most popular content on your site, either posts or pages. This is very important, as it shows you what is popular with your readers, and you can use this information to help you decide what kind of content to create next. The next box shows you the Search Engine Terms and phrases visitors use to find your site when they search online. Again, this is an important metric, as you can see what search terms users are searching to get to your site, and you can then do further keyword research to find related search terms that you can rank for in the search engines. The Clicks box shows you the number of visitors that clicked any outbound links on your site. The Subscription box at the bottom shows you the number of interactions with your content on your site.

Monitoring your site's visitor statistics is an important part of your site maintenance. When you are fully engaged with the stats of your site, you are in the best position to decide on the best course of action. When you first check your site's stats, you might feel a little depressed by the numbers, and you see that you have no or few visitors to your site. Don't be discouraged as you are not alone in this. This is a stage that all websites go through - even the top blog sites that get millions of visitors a month once had no or very few visitors. As long as you keep on pumping out excellent content and you follow best SEO practices, you will soon be getting visitors in large number but as with many things in life, a little patience and perseverance will go a long way.

I want to outline some important site statistics that you should monitor on your blog, as there is a wealth of information in them and this can really help you to take your site to the next level.

1. No. of overall visitors. This is the metric that stands out the most, and the one that people generally use to measure how successful a website is. With this metric, you need to make sure that you track the general trend. Ask yourself this question: are visitor numbers on the increase or decrease? Also, make sure to find out the reasons behind either the increase or decrease of visitors. It could be to do with how frequently you post, promotion strategies, topics, etc.

2. Most popular posts and pages. This metric will show you what is popular on your site - what posts are being read the most. Really dissecting the details of this metric is a gold mine, as it gives you clear pointers on what kind of topics to write more on; it shows you what posts and pages that you can further optimize and additional internal links to other content on your site.

3. Which sites are sending the most traffic? You can learn what sites are showing you love and sending you traffic. Knowing this will help you to build a relationship with the owner of that site to make sure that they continue to send traffic your way.

4. What keywords are visitors using to get to your site? Most websites get their traffic from search engines, and knowing what keywords visitors are using to get to your site is extremely important. This will help to optimize your site further, by adding the keywords appropriate to your content. You can use this information when creating more content for your site.

5. Outbound clicks. Online readers are like explorers; they constantly move from site to site depending on what they are looking for. When you know what outbound links your visitors are clicking, it will help you understand what kind of content your visitors want more of.

When you first create a website, it is at the early stages of its lifecycle. This is the period where you need to create more content and optimize your site for SEO. The site stats feature available in the Jetpack plug-in will be sufficient for your needs early on but as your site grows and the number of visitors increase, you will need an advanced tool to analyze your site's statistics, and what better tool to use than Google Analytics. You really must add this very powerful tool to your arsenal in the future, as it will help you to number crunch every aspect of your sites statistics.

Chapter 11: Practical Tips To Create A Successful Blog

The universal law of cause and effect says that every effect has a cause and there are no effects without a cause, even if we don't know what the cause is. This is the basis of all scientific research. You're probably wondering what this has to do with creating a successful blog. Well, the answer to that is simple - copy success. I don't mean literally copy and plagiarize other successful bloggers but copy their techniques and strategies to get the same results. One thing that is known for sure is that if you follow what a successful person does, you will also be successful, and the same is true when creating a blog. Success leaves tracks, and the masters in the blogging business have left clear tracks for you to follow. In this chapter, I want to outline some basic tips that you can use which have been proven to get results.

Find your passion

When you first start out in the blogosphere community, the first thing that you should do is find a suitable topic that you want to blog about. When you want to create a blog, you need to have a topic that will be the focus of your online content. It is worth noting here that the topic you choose will directly affect your website's traffic potential and overall success. The process of choosing a topic can be quite overwhelming for those who have never created a website before, but if you follow some simple guidelines, it is actually very straightforward. In today's blogosphere community, you are likely to find that the blog topic or niche that you want to create a blog for will have blogs that are dedicated to that niche.

Therefore, it is important that you think through this part very carefully, because the blogging landscape has completely changed over the last decade; it is considerably more difficult to become popular, stand out from the crowd or capitalize on success. In the early days of the web, if you blogged about a topic such as sports or politics you could easily get a large following, but in today's environment the landscape is very different. There are extremely popular and authoritative blogs on sports and politics that would make it very hard for you to even get a sniff in niches like these. The important thing to do here is to research the niche that you want to create a blog about thoroughly first before doing anything else. You might find that you are better off starting a blog related to the financial side of the restaurant business than you are to creating a blog on general finance.

If you look at the most successful websites on the Internet and their authors, you will find that they have passion for their topics. When you are writing about something that you love, you are more likely to be successful instead of writing about a topic that you have no passion for or know little about it. Also, newbies often make the mistake of choosing a topic that is very profitable, but that is not their passion and in most cases their websites tend to fail as their lack of passion and knowledge is reflected on the content of their websites. It is worth focusing on a niche that might not have high demand, but you can build enough traffic that will enable you to profit from your topic.

When choosing a topic, avoid the broad topics like making money, shopping and food; try to narrow down to a niche. Broad topics are searched for millions of times per month and the competition is very strong. Instead of creating a website on exotic holiday locations, you could create a website for a particular destination such as Anguilla beaches - this way you have narrowed a niche and there is likely to be less competition.

Do your homework: keyword Research

The first step in choosing a topic is to do keyword research on the topic that you want to create a website for. Keyword research is now an important part of the website creation process as there is so much saturation on almost every topic. You need to refine the supply and demand for the choice of topic. If you target the correct keywords, you will be ranked in major search engines and will subsequently generate good traffic to your website. The simple task of keyword research is to find a topic that has good demand and minimal supply, as this will give you a good chance to rank well with the search engines. There are many tools online that you can use to conduct your keyword research. These include:

- Google keyword planner
- Market Samurai

To use the Google keyword planner tool, you just need to have an active Google account and you can login here: https://adwords.google.com/KeywordPlanner. Market samurai is pretty much the same as the Google keyword planner tool; it uses your Google account to get the search metrics from Google. The main difference with the keyword planner tool is that it gives you a detailed breakdown of the keywords that you want to target. Market Samurai will give you a list of all of the top ten sites that are competing for high page ranking. It has built-in stats that tell you if a particular keyword is highly competitive and whether you should be targeting that keyword. But, above all the main difference is that the Google keyword planner is free, and Market Samurai will cost you $149, correct at the time of this writing - http://www.marketsamurai.com/full-version/. The Google keyword planner at this stage should be sufficient for your needs, but don't completely dismiss Market Samurai, as it can give you detailed breakdown for a specific keyword that you want to target, and it is better suited when you are embarking on a large project to use as your keyword research tool.

When you perform analysis of a keyword with these tools, they will help you to understand the supply and demand for a particular keyword and its associated topic. One of the great features about these tools is that they reveal how many times a particular keyword was searched for in the last month.

Supply

In general, the business term supply refers to the number of websites that cater to a particular keyword. This means that these sites will have that keyword mentioned several times on their website to attract search engine traffic. When you are doing your initial research, you should look closely at the results displayed on the search engine; if we search on Google for *shoes*, it will display the number of websites that mention the word *shoes* on their website:

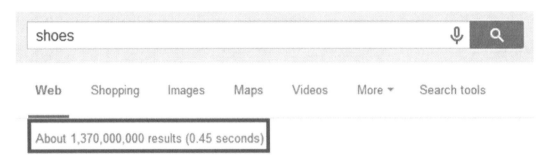

From the screenshot above, the results are quite large - 1.3 billion websites. This doesn't mean that all of these websites are focusing on this phrase alone, but it shows you how many websites mention this keyword on their sites. The first few results are the most targeted, as they will contain the information that a user is looking for. A technique that you can use to narrow down the number of results is to use the *intitle* query. So if you type: *intitle: Shoes* the number of results will go down significantly. In this search, Google has found 1.36 million:

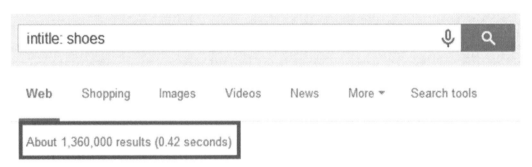

We mentioned previously that it is important to narrow down a niche; *shoes* is very broad. If we search for *walking boots,* the results also drop quite significantly compared to the general shoe keyword, as we have now narrowed down the niche:

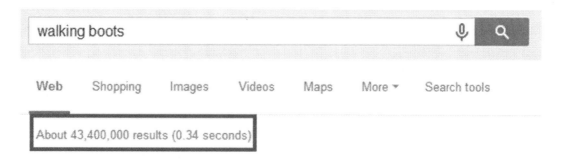

Demand

In simple terms, the demand is the number of people looking for a particular product, service or information. In our situation, it is the number of people searching online for your idea or topic by using keywords. You can check demand using useful tools such as the Google keyword planner which is a free and powerful tool.

If we wanted to find out the demand for walking boots, we would type these two words into the Google keyword planner and it would return the number of times it was searched for, plus the competition for this keyword:

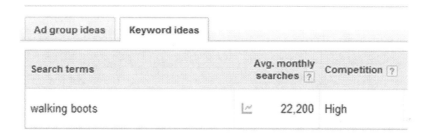

From the results, we can see that there is high competition for this phrase and that it has been searched for quite a lot – competition here refers to the number of advertisers that will buy Google adwords for that keyword. Typically, the more popular and profitable a keyword the higher the competition. In the Ad group ideas tab, the keyword planner tool gives you suggestions related to the keyword that you are researching, which is also being searched by visitors:

Ad group (by relevance)	Keywords	Avg. monthly searches	Competition
Keywords like: ...	walking boot, za...	8,160	High
Women Walking.	walking boots fo...	24,970	High
Men Walking (12)	mens walking b...	15,210	High
Sale Walking (11)	walking boots s...	2,710	High
Waterproof Wal...	waterproof walki...	4,730	High
Best Boots (34)	best walking bo...	23,500	High

Long Tail Keywords

When you are carrying out your initial research and you see words that have 500 or even 5000 searches a day, you might get excited and start targeting keywords like this; however, the reality is that exact and popular search terms only make up 30% of the searches performed online. This leaves a massive 70% as the long tail keyword. Long Tail keywords contain unique searches that are performed looking for specific things. So, you might have someone performing a long tail keyword search such as: 'best price air jordan size 12'. This person is ready to buy and is looking for the best price. Long tail keywords can generate good profit in terms of both traffic and money for your website.

It is always worth noting that there is no such thing as the perfect topic that has the highest demand and no supply! There will always be competition and you just have to make sure that you stand out from the crowd. This can be done with a simple yet overlooked concept: **quality content**. I put these two words in bold to emphasize their importance because once you have quality content that engages and your visitors can trust you, this trust will convert into more traffic. Also, the content can only be of the highest quality if you enjoy writing about your topic with passion, this will show in your writing. The biggest mistake that newcomers often make is to choose a topic because it is associated with expensive products or services yet they have no passion for or little knowledge in the subject matter. Choose a topic that you enjoy but at the same time, have enough demand to warrant your commitment.

Come up with solutions and you will be successful

People that are online searching for information usually have a problem and are looking for a solution. If you can come up with a solution to their problems, you will be very successful and you can build trust, loyalty, and credibility - all very important to a website owner. Successful bloggers write a post that solves a problem that readers have and they focus on this aspect when blogging. When you solve problems, you'll make an impression on people; readers will return to your blog and they will be inclined to share your content and tell others.

How to identify problems to solve

To come up with solutions to problems that people are experiencing, you need to first find out how to solve the problem yourself first. It is human nature that the problem you are experiencing is also affecting others. One of the best ways to identify problems is to first identify your own current problems and then find out how to solve them. This is the basis for coming up with solutions because you are in the best position to offer advice in how to solve that particular problem.

Write a list post

In the world of blogs, competition is always fierce and you need to grab your reader's attention. The best way to do this is to use what is called a list post. A list post will list the items in a post as a numbered list. For example, the post title "10 ways to beat the high cost of living" is more effective at grabbing the reader's attention than "how to beat the cost of living". Readers love these kinds of posts because it makes a very specific promise of what is in store for the reader. When you deliver with quality content, you'll not only have a satisfied reader, but a potential sharing of your post to their social contacts and therefore more exposure for your site and content.

Write eye catching headlines

Whenever you visit a website, one of the striking things are the headlines. Many people subscribe to WordPress sites using RSS readers that only show the headline. So your headlines are very important. The following are tips for writing impactful headlines:

Use benefit rich statements

People always have the question: 'what's in it for me?' so you need to tell them just how they will benefit from reading your post. In the shoes example, instead of writing *Walking boots*, you could write *Walking boots that are good for your back!* This will grab the reader's attention as you have informed them how they will benefit from your post.

Ask a question
You can grab a user's attention by using a question as the headline, e.g. *'Would you like to know how to get rid of back pain easily without treatment?'* This will encourage readers to read the post and respond.

Add humor
Adding humor to your headline will create personality for your readership and it makes dull and boring subjects worthwhile when reading them. But, you have to be careful as you don't want to offend anyone or come across as corny.

Incorporate the word 'you' into your content
As readers go through your posts and headlines, they want to feel part of the discussion at hand and the word 'you' gives it a personal touch.

Add real life and personal events
When you write about personal life events that are related to your topic and niche ,it will add personality to your content and you will build good user relationships. Readers will start to trust you. When you write about personal events such as meetings that you have attended or people that you met, it will engage readers and remind them that the person behind the website and content is a real human being just like them.

Hold contests
Having regular contests on your website will help you build loyalty. Everyone would like to take part in a competition and win something. You should aim to make them easy to enter and offer prizes that your readers will value. The key is to make your contests are easy to enter; if it is difficult to enter, people won't bother. The prize value should reflect the tasks that the entrants have to do.

Learn from the pros
This is understood, but to be successful in almost anything you must learn from the pros. Creating a successful blog is no different. You can learn so much from bloggers at the top of their game in such a short time, in comparison to learning from your own experience. The first step is to identify a successful blog in your niche. This is probably going to be obvious to you, but you might still need to do some research. Once you have pinpointed the blog that you want to analyze, you want to observe carefully, and make note of the following things:

- What topics are they covering?
- Are they ignoring certain topics?
- What topics are the most popular?
- What is the frequency of posting? Daily, Weekly, biweekly, Monthly?

The purpose of this exercise is to identify what is working well on this popular blog, and then try to find anything that the site is not covering or not covering well. Then, use this opportunity to fill the gaps with your blog. When you analyze blogs in your niche, you get to understand what works well in your niche, and what opportunities there are to fill any gaps left by these blogs on your own blog. Remember what I said at the beginning - you should copy success. What I mean by this is that you should copy what they did, not their content or replicate every aspect of another blog. There is a wealth of knowledge and strategies that you can learn from top blogs but always make sure that you differentiate yourself and that you are unique. Also, it is important not to get too carried away when doing this task. By spending too much time analyzing your competitors, you won't focus on what is important, which is creating great content and optimizing your site for SEO.

Conclusion

The Wordpress story will continue to dominate the online space for years to come, and this is means that the platform will only get better. In just ten years Wordpress has become the CMS to use for creating a website, who know in a few years' time what new features that Wordpress will have! I hope that you enjoyed reading my book.

Feedback

As a qualified teacher of IT I have always been taught to be reflective, and look for ways to improve. My journey in creating this book on Wordpress was like delivering a lesson in a classroom, and as well as one does in executing an excellent lesson there is always room for improvement. I would like to hear your honest feedback on my book, and if you think that I can improve on any aspect, then please take a minute to complete this simple form: http://expresstuts.com/feedback on my website, and I promise to improve any areas or aspects of the book. If you have enjoyed reading this book, then I would kindly like to ask you to leave a review, to let others know – it will only take you a few minutes, and I will be forever grateful!

More Wordpress resources

With Wordpress there is so much support and resources available online, just performing a quick search on Google will yield literally thousands of results for you to choose from. Some are better than others and you have to sift through the results and determine which ones are good. The official Wordpress headquarters at Wordpress.org has lots of resources available and you will also find a very active community in the forums. So, in terms of more resources I recommend:

1. http://www.Wordpress.org

2. http://www.Expresstuts.com

3. Google search for your Wordpress query

Terms of use and disclaimer

The author and publisher of this book and the accompanying materials have used their best efforts in preparing this book. The author and publisher make no representation or warranties with respect to the accuracy, applicability, fitness, or completeness of the contents of this book. The information contained in this book is strictly for educational purposes. Therefore, if you wish to apply ideas contained in this book, you are taking full responsibility for your actions. The author and publisher disclaim any warranties (express or implied), merchantability, or fitness for any particular purpose. The author and publisher shall in no event be held liable to any party for any direct, indirect, punitive, special, incidental or other consequential damages arising directly or indirectly from any use of this material, which is provided "as is", and without warranties. The author and publisher do not warrant the performance, effectiveness or applicability of any sites listed or linked to in this book.

All links are for information purposes only and are not warranted for content, accuracy or any other implied or explicit purpose. This book is © copyrighted by Zak Cagaros and is protected under the US Copyright Act of 1976 and all other applicable international, federal, state and local laws, with ALL rights reserved. No part of this may be copied, or changed in any format, sold, or used in any way other than what is outlined within this book under any circumstances without express permission from Zak Cagaros.

Made in the USA
San Bernardino, CA
04 June 2015